MORE
MIDDLE SCHOOL
TALKSHEETS
ON THE NEW TESTAMENT
FOR AGES 11-14

52 READY-TO-USE DISCUSSIONS

DAVID LYNN

youth
specialties

ZONDERVAN.com/
AUTHORTRACKER
follow your favorite authors

ZONDERVAN

More Middle School Talksheets on the New Testament, Epic Bible Stories: 52 Ready-to-Use Discussions
Copyright © 2010 by David Lynn

YS Youth Specialties is a trademark of YOUTHWORKS!, INCORPORATED and is registered with the United States Patent and Trademark Office.

Requests for information should be addressed to:

Zondervan, *Grand Rapids, Michigan 49530*

ISBN 978-0-310-66870-1

Cover design: David Conn
Interior design: Brandi Etheredge Design

Printed in the United States of America

14 15 /DCI/ 23 22 21 20 19 18 17 16 15 14 13 12 11 10 9 8 7 6 5

For Megan:
Blessing #2

CONTENTS

THE HOWS AND WHATS OF TALKSHEETS

You are holding a very valuable book! No, it won't make you a genius or millionaire. But it does contain 52 instant discussions for middle school youth. Inside you'll find reproducible NEW TESTAMENT TalkSheets that cover 52 stories from the birth of Jesus to the end of the book of Revelation; plus simple, step-by-step instructions on how to use them. All you need is this book, a few copies of the handouts, and some young people (and maybe a snack or two). You're on your way to touching on some serious issues in young people's lives today.

These NEW TESTAMENT TalkSheets are user-friendly and very flexible. They can be used in a youth group meeting, a Sunday school class, or a Bible study group. You can adapt them for either large or small groups. And, they can be covered in only 20 minutes or explored more intensively in two hours.

You can build an entire youth group meeting around a single NEW TESTAMENT TalkSheet, or you can use NEW TESTAMENT TalkSheets to supplement other materials and resources you might be using. These are tools for you—how you use them is your choice.

Middle School NEW TESTAMENT TalkSheets are not your average curriculum or workbook. This collection of discussions will get your young people involved and excited about talking through important issues. The NEW TESTAMENT TalkSheets deal with epic stories and include interesting activities, challenging questions, and eye-catching graphics. They will challenge your young people to think about opinions, learn about themselves, and grow in their faith.

IMPORTANT GUIDING PRINCIPLES BEFORE USING NEW TESTAMENT TALKSHEETS

Let's begin by agreeing on two primary principles: (1) Faith is essentially caught, not taught, and (2) The Holy Spirit alone works best to establish faith within someone's life, changing someone from a knower to a believer and a church attendee to a lifelong follower of Jesus. If we can agree on these first principles, then it is easier to explain how NEW TESTAMENT TalkSheets are designed. It is not so much a teaching tool as a tool designed to engage real faith connections and encourage faith vocabulary in the lives of young people.

So many church attendees do not know how to articulate their faith, nor do they often see real, vital connections for their faith outside of the church building. NEW TESTAMENT TalkSheets exercises are designed to help young people make real-life connections between what they believe and their day-to-day lives, as well as develop a living faith vocabulary, as opposed to a church vocabulary used only in the God house to please adults and religious leaders. For faith to grow with us in ways that last a lifetime, all of us need to discover faith's vital connection in our day-to-day lives. We need to see where Jesus in our lives engages the real world we live in. And we need to have an ability to express this connection, or a "vocabulary of faith" that grows with us and goes with us, rather than merely a religious Christian-ese we speak in religious settings and on certain occasions.

These NEW TESTAMENT TalkSheets exercises are aimed at engaging young people in real conversations where belief can be discovered, Christian words and notions can be unpacked, and faith can be connected with and expressed. In such settings the earliest Christians explored and expressed their faith. Our Lord Jesus used fishing with fishermen to connect his first followers with what he was doing, using words and images that were familiar to them. Creating settings where young people can talk about faith develops a faith vocabulary and deepens faith by connecting it to relevant life experiences.

NEW TESTAMENT TALKSHEETS AS AN ENGAGING TOOL RATHER THAN A TEACHING TOOL

We have often made a very fundamental mistake in how we assist young people in their faith development. We have hammered down on the obvious answers to questions that the young people are often not even asking. What you wind up with are young people who can answer the question "correctly" but don't see why the answer is relevant to their daily lives.

Take, for example, the primary question of faith: Who is your Lord and Savior? The right answer is "Jesus Christ is my Lord and Savior." I have heard young people answer this question correctly for many years. But when it comes to real life, I have also witnessed many young people get stumped on a valid understanding as to what "Lord" means in a culture where all people are their own sources of truth or as to why they need to be saved when all people are "basically okay." We often make the mistake of assuming that good information is enough. But the information needs to possess something vital for youth to attach to, and if the questions are not there, the information may not seem relevant.

When we teach young people answers to questions they are not asking, nor even know that they need to ask, we are leaving them with answers that don't fit and faith that will not stand up under pressure. This is why we believe that young people need to understand the tensions of life from which questions arise and struggle with how they answer those questions daily in their lives before they hear how God has addressed those questions in the person of Jesus Christ. Then we can ask, "If this is how life is, then who is YOUR Lord and Savior?"

By engaging young people inwardly and INNER-gizing young people into a real dialogue about their life, perceptions, and faith, we can make pathways where we can partner with them as they grow in their discipleship.

A COMMON PITFALL TO AVOID

Faith development is often a stepped process. Some things need to be set in place before other things can be embraced. We might say that a person moves from A to B before moving on to C and eventually arriving at D. A mistake many leaders may make is that the movement from A to D looks simple to them, and they are impatient for those they are working with to make that developmental leap. Good Christian leadership understands that we are often guides for encounters on the roadside as people make their way in following the Master.

A pitfall that is common in Christian leadership is to invite people to make a leap in faith development they're unable to sustain. Often young believers make a substitutional leap of faith and jump from A to D based on what the leader believes. People are very willing to do this because they might trust their leaders or might be afraid to express real doubts in an unsafe environment. They might also think it's a lack on their part to move so slowly in faith, which can make them feel guilty. There's also performance anxiety in our faith settings that can cause people to take on language that fits the situation but is essentially not a part of their day-to-day lives.

I have witnessed these conditions, where real faith is not deep enough to sustain the pressures of real life and substitutional faith is worn like a garment in the God house. Such followers who attend gatherings but cannot pray for themselves hold a secret sense of doubt and guilt and often defer to the religious leadership on all matters of faith.

Jesus spoke of such followers, who are like shallow soil on which the seed falls.

Essentially there are three roles a discussion leader can fulfill: An Instrument, a Thorn, or a Stage Director: (1) An Instrument can be a force in the hand of the Holy Spirit that works in the process of faith-building in the life of young disciples; (2) As a Thorn the leader can become an irritant in the life of disciples that alienates them from the faith community by creating an unsafe faith environment with unrealistic expectations and impatient discipleship methods; (3) A Stage Director leader is one who inoculates young people against catching real faith by creating an environment that encourages satisfying an expectation by taking on a mask of believing and a language of the church. This effectually insulates them from embracing real, vital faith expressed in a living language. As you can see, only one role serves well in the life of young followers, and that is the role of an Instrument.

NEW TESTAMENT TALKSHEETS HELPS US BE GOOD STEWARDS OF A SACRED PROCESS

But if we understand deep, rich soil may take time and much mulching if a seed is to take root, then we can as leaders trust that faith is not about ourselves achieving something in the life of a person, but about the Holy Spirit shaping a life into a follower. We can become stewards of a most sacred process. Young people can pick up useless notions of faith and life on their way to discovering real faith that rumbles deep with a vital discipleship. Patient and loving mentoring is needed if these useless notions are to be replaced with life-giving awareness in a living, vital faith in Jesus.

Remember that Thomas did not at first believe that Jesus was resurrected even though the other disciples expressed to him what they had witnessed. It is a great testimony of those early followers of Jesus that Thomas was still with them "in

their midst" a week later when Jesus showed up and confirmed himself to Thomas. It is important to create a safe environment where young people can explore their faith and express themselves without the expectation of correct performance or the need to make the developmental leap that they are not ready to sustain as a disciple until, for them, Jesus shows up.

LEADING A NEW TESTAMENT TALKSHEET DISCUSSION

NEW TESTAMENT TalkSheets can be used as a curriculum for your youth group, but they are designed to be springboards for discussion. They encourage your young people to take part and interact with each other while talking about real life issues. And hopefully they'll do some serious thinking, discover new ideas for themselves, defend their points of view, and make decisions.

Youth today face a world of moral confusion. Youth leaders must teach the church's beliefs and values—and also help young people make the right choices in a world full of options. Teenagers are bombarded with the voices of society and the media—most of which drown out what they hear from the church.

A NEW TESTAMENT TalkSheet discussion works for this very reason. While dealing with the questions and activities on the NEW TESTAMENT TalkSheet, your young people will think carefully about issues, compare their beliefs and values with others, and make their own choices. NEW TESTAMENT TalkSheets will challenge your group to explain and rework their ideas in a Christian atmosphere of acceptance, support, and growth.

The most common fear of middle school youth group leaders is, "What will I do if the young people in my group just sit there and don't say anything?" Well, when young people don't have anything to say, it's because they haven't had a chance or time to get their thoughts organized! Most young people haven't developed the ability to think on their feet. Since many are afraid they might sound stupid, they don't know how to voice their ideas and opinions.

The solution? NEW TESTAMENT TalkSheets let your youth deal with the issues in a challenging, non-threatening way before the actual discussion begins. They'll have time to organize their thoughts, write them down, and ease their fears about participating. They may even look forward to sharing their answers! Most importantly, they'll want to find out what others say and open up to talk through the topics.

If you're still a little leery about the success of a real discussion among your youth, that's okay!

YOUR ROLE AS THE LEADER

The best discussions don't happen by accident. They require careful preparation and a sensitive leader. Don't worry if you aren't experienced or don't have hours to prepare. NEW TESTAMENT TalkSheets are designed to help even the novice leader! The more NEW TESTAMENT TalkSheet discussions you lead, the easier it becomes. Keep the following tips in mind when using the NEW TESTAMENT TalkSheets as you get your young people talking.

BE CHOOSY

Each NEW TESTAMENT TalkSheet deals with a different story. Under the title of each of the NEW TESTAMENT TalkSheets is a simple subtitle heading that expresses the theme of the TalkSheet. Choose a NEW TESTAMENT TalkSheet based on the needs and the maturity level of your group. Don't feel obligated to use the NEW TESTAMENT TalkSheets in the order they appear in this book. Use your best judgment and mix them up however you want—they're tools for you!

MAKE COPIES

Young people will need their own copy of the TalkSheet. Only make copies of the youth side of the TalkSheet! The material on the reverse side (the leader's guide) is just for you. You're able to make copies for your group because we have given you permission to do so. U.S. copyright laws have not changed, and it is still mandatory to request permission from a publisher before making copies of other published material. It is against the law not to do so. However, permission is given for you to make copies of this material for your group only, not for every youth group in your state. Thank you for cooperating.

TRY IT YOURSELF

Once you have chosen a NEW TESTAMENT TalkSheet for your group, answer the questions and do the activities yourself. Imagine your young people's reactions to the NEW TESTAMENT TalkSheet. This will help you prepare for the discussion and understand what you are asking them to do. Plus, you'll have some time to think of other appropriate questions, activities, and Bible verses.

GET SOME INSIGHT

On each leader's guide page, you'll find numerous tips and ideas for getting the most out of your discussion. You may want to add some of your own thoughts or ideas in the margins.

INTRODUCE THE TOPIC

You may introduce the topic before you pass out the NEW TESTAMENT TalkSheets to your group, and then allow the topic to develop as you use the material. We have a simple format on the leader's guide that can help your introduction. First, there is the "Read Out Loud" section. Simply read the paragraph or two out loud, then ask a young person to read the story from the Bible. After the story is read, you can use the question in the "Ask" section to get the group primed for a discussion of the story.

NEW TESTAMENT TalkSheets work best with a strong concluding presentation rather than a strong teaching time prior to using the Talksheet. You can use the "Close" section to help guide your closing presentation. Depending on your group, keep your introduction short and to the point. Be careful not to over-introduce the topic, sound preachy, or resolve the issue before you've started. Your goal is to spark their interest and leave plenty of room for discussion, allowing the material to introduce the topic.

Pass out the NEW TESTAMENT TalkSheet and be sure that everyone has a pencil or pen. Now you're on your way! The following are excellent methods you can use to introduce any topic in this book—

- Show a related short film or video.
- Read a passage from a book or magazine that relates to the subject.
- Play a popular CD that deals with the topic.
- Perform a short skit or dramatic presentation.
- Play a simulation game or role-play, setting up the topic.
- Present current statistics or survey results, or read a current newspaper article that provides recent information about the topic.
- Use an icebreaker or other crowd game, getting into the topic in a humorous way.
- Use posters, videos, or any other visuals to help focus attention on the topic.

There are endless possibilities for an intro— you're limited only by your own creativity! Keep in mind that a clear and simple introduction is a very important part of each session.

SET BOUNDARIES
It'll be helpful to set a few ground rules before the discussion. Keep the rules to a minimum, of course, but let the youth know what's expected of them. Here are suggestions for some basic ground rules:
- What's said in this room stays in this room. Emphasize the importance of confidentiality.

Some young people will open up; some won't. Confidentiality is vital for a good discussion. If your youth can't keep the discussion in the room, then they won't open up.
- No put-downs. Mutual respect is important. If your young people disagree with some opinions, ask them to comment on the subject (but not on the other person).
- There's no such thing as a dumb question. Your group members must feel free to ask questions at any time. The best way to learn is to ask questions and get answers.
- No one is forced to talk. Let everyone know they have the right to pass or not answer any question.
- Only one person speaks at a time. This is a mutual respect issue. Everyone's opinion is worthwhile and deserves to be heard.

Communicate with your group that everyone needs to respect these boundaries. If you sense that your group members are attacking each other or getting a negative attitude during the discussion, do stop and deal with the problem before going on.

ALLOW ENOUGH TIME
Pass out copies of the NEW TESTAMENT TalkSheet to your young people after the introduction and make sure that each person has a pen or pencil and a Bible. There are usually five or six activities on each NEW TESTAMENT TalkSheet. If your time is limited, or if you are using only a part of the NEW TESTAMENT TalkSheet, tell the group to complete only the activities you assign.

Decide ahead of time whether or not you would like the young people to work on the NEW TESTAMENT TalkSheet individually or in groups.

Let them know how much time they have for completing the NEW TESTAMENT TalkSheet and let them know when there is a minute (or so) left. Go ahead and give them some extra time, and then start the discussion when everyone seems ready to go.

SET THE STAGE

Create a climate of acceptance. Most teenagers are afraid to voice their opinions because they don't want to be laughed at or look stupid in front of their peers. They want to feel safe if they're going to share their feelings and beliefs. Communicate that they can share their thoughts and ideas—even if they may be different or unpopular. If your young people get put-downs, criticism, laughter, or snide comments (even if their statements are opposed to the teachings of the Bible), it'll hurt the discussion.

Always phrase your questions—even those that are printed on the NEW TESTAMENT TalkSheets—so that you are asking for an opinion, not an answer. For example, if a question reads, "What should Bill have done in that situation?" the simple addition of the three words "do you think" makes the question less threatening and a matter of opinion, rather than a demand for the right answer. Your young people will relax when they feel more comfortable and confident. Plus, they'll know that you actually care about their opinions and they'll feel appreciated!

LEAD THE DISCUSSION

Discuss the NEW TESTAMENT TalkSheet with the group and encourage all your young people to participate. Communicate that it's important for them to respect each other's opinions and feelings! The more they contribute, the better the discussion will be.

If your youth group is big, you may divide it into smaller groups of six to 12. Each of these small groups should have a facilitator—either an adult leader or a youth member—to keep the discussion going. Remind the facilitators not to dominate. If the group looks to the facilitator for an answer, ask him or her to direct the questions or responses back to the group. Once the smaller groups have completed their discussions, combine them into one large group and ask the different groups to share their ideas.

You don't have to divide the groups up with every NEW TESTAMENT TalkSheet. For some discus-sions, you may want to vary the group size and/or divide the meeting into groups of the same sex.

The discussion should target the questions and answers on the NEW TESTAMENT TalkSheet. Go through them one at a time and ask the young people to share their responses. Have them compare their answers and brainstorm new ones in addition to the ones they've written down. Encourage them to share their opinions and answers, but don't force those who are quiet.

AFFIRM ALL RESPONSES—RIGHT OR WRONG

Let your young people know that their comments and contributions are appreciated and important. This is especially true for those who rarely speak dur-ing group activities. Make a point of thanking them for joining in. This will be an incentive for them to participate further.

Remember that affirmation doesn't mean approval. Affirm even those comments that seem wrong to you. You'll show that everyone has a right to express their ideas—no matter how controversial they may be. If someone states an opinion that is off base, make a mental note of the comment. Then in your wrap-up, come back to the comment or present a different point of view in a positive way. But don't reprimand the person who voiced the comment.

DON'T BE THE AUTHORITATIVE ANSWER

Some young people think you have the right to answer to every question. They'll look to you for approval, even when they are answering another group member's question. If they start to focus on you for answers, redirect them toward the group by making a comment like, "Remember that you're talking to everyone, not just me."

Your goal as the facilitator is to keep the discus-sion alive and kicking. It's important that your young people think of you as a member of the group—on their level. The less authoritative you are, the more value your own opinions will have. If your young people view you as a peer, they will listen to your comments. You have a tremendous responsibility to be, with sincerity, their trusted friend.

LISTEN TO EACH PERSON

God gave you one mouth and two ears. Good discussion leaders know how to listen. Although it's tempting at times, don't monopolize the discussion. Encourage others to talk first—then express your opinions during your wrap-up.

DON'T FORCE IT

Encourage all your young people to talk, but don't make them comment. Each member has the right to pass. If you feel that the discussion isn't going well, go on to the next question or restate the question to keep them moving.

DON'T TAKE SIDES

You'll probably have different opinions expressed in the group from time to time. Be extra careful not to take one side or another. Encourage both sides to think through their positions—ask questions to get them deeper. If everyone agrees on an issue, you can play devil's advocate with tough questions and stretch their thinking. Remain neutral—your point of view is your own, not that of the group.

DON'T LET ANYONE (INCLUDING YOU) TAKE OVER

Nearly every youth group has one person who likes to talk and is perfectly willing to express an opinion on any subject. Try to encourage equal participation from all the young people.

SET UP FOR THE TALK

Make sure that the seating arrangement is inclusive and encourages a comfortable, safe atmosphere for discussion. Theater-style seating (in rows) isn't discussion-friendly. Instead, arrange the chairs in a circle or semicircle (or sit on the floor with pillows).

LET THEM LAUGH!

Discussions can be fun! Most of the NEW TESTAMENT TalkSheets include questions that'll make them laugh and get them thinking, too.

LET THEM BE SILENT

Silence can be scary for discussion leaders! Some react by trying to fill the silence with a question or comment. The following suggestions may help you to handle silence more effectively:

- Be comfortable with silence. Wait it out for 30 seconds or so before responding. You may want to restate the question to give your young people a gentle nudge.
- Talk about the silence with the group. What does the silence mean? Do they really not have any comments? Maybe they're confused or embarrassed or don't want to share.
- Answer the silence with questions or comments like, "I know this is challenging to think about…" or "It's scary to be the first to talk." If you acknowledge the silence, it may break the ice.
- Ask a different question that may be easier to handle or that will clarify the one already posed. But don't do this too quickly without giving them time to think the first one through.

KEEP IT UNDER CONTROL

Monitor the discussion. Be aware if the discussion is going in a certain direction or off track. This can happen fast, especially if the young people disagree or things get heated. Mediate wisely and set the tone that you want. If your group gets bored with an issue, get them back on track. Let the discussion unfold, but be sensitive to your group and who is or is not getting involved.

If a young person brings up a side issue that's interesting, decide whether or not to pursue it. If discussion is going well and the issue is worth discussion, let them talk it through. But, if things get way off track, say something like, "Let's come back to that subject later if we have time. Right now, let's finish our discussion on…"

BE CREATIVE AND FLEXIBLE

You don't have to follow the order of the questions on the NEW TESTAMENT TalkSheet. Follow your own creative instinct. If you find other ways to use the NEW TESTAMENT TalkSheets, use them! Go ahead and add other questions or Bible references.

Don't feel pressured to spend time on every single activity. If you're short on time, you can skip some items. Stick with the questions that are the most interesting to the group.

SET YOUR GOALS

NEW TESTAMENT TalkSheets are designed to move along toward a goal, but you need to identify your goal in advance. What would you like your young people to learn? What truth should they discover? What is the goal of the session? If you don't know where you're going, it's doubtful you will get there. As stated earlier, there is a theme for each of the NEW TESTAMENT TalkSheets. You will find this theme in smaller type in the heading of each of the TalkSheet titles.

BE THERE FOR YOUR YOUNG PEOPLE

Some young people may want to talk more with you (you got 'em thinking!). Let them know that you can talk one-on-one with them afterward.

Communicate to the young people that they can feel free to talk with you about anything with confidentiality. Let them know you're there for them with support and concern, even after the NEW TESTAMENT TalkSheet discussion has been completed.

CLOSE THE DISCUSSION

There is a "Close" section at the end of each of the leader guides with a paragraph or two of closing comments. Present a challenge to the group by asking yourself, "What do I want the young people to remember most from this discussion?" There's your wrap up!

Sometimes you won't need a wrap-up. You may want to leave the issue hanging and discuss it in another meeting. That way, your group can think about it more and you can nail down the final ideas later.

A FINAL WORD TO THE WISE— THAT'S YOU!

Some of these NEW TESTAMENT TalkSheets deal with topics that may be sensitive or controversial for your young people. You're encouraging discussion and inviting your young people to express their opinions. As a result, parents or others in your church may criticize you—they may not see the importance of such discussions. Use your best judgment. If you suspect that a particular NEW TESTAMENT TalkSheet will cause problems, you may not want to use it. Or you may want to tweak a particular NEW TESTAMENT TalkSheet and only cover some of the questions. Either way, the potential bad could outweigh the good—better safe than sorry. To avoid any misunderstanding, you may want to give the parents or senior pastor (or whomever else you are accountable to) copies of the NEW TESTAMENT TalkSheet before you use it. Let them know the discussion you would like to have and the goal you are hoping to accomplish. Challenge your young people to take their NEW TESTAMENT TalkSheet home to talk about it with their parents. How would their parents, as young people, have answered the questions? Your young people may find that their parents understand them better than they thought. Also, encourage them to think of other Bible verses or ways that the NEW TESTAMENT TalkSheet applies to their lives.

1. Luke 2:8-20

THE SHEPHERDS & THE ANGELS

Part of worship is experiencing the presence of God

1. What do you think surprised the shepherds the most?

___ The scary presence of angels
___ The fact that God had come to earth as a baby
   born into poverty
___ The arrival of Jesus, their Savior
___ The brightness of God's glory
___ The smell of the sheep

2. If you were one of the shepherds who heard this good news, what would it make you want to do?

• Run and hide
• Run out and tell others
• Pinch myself to see if I was dreaming
• Wonder if it was something I ate
• Ask if the message could be repeated
• Stand up and cheer

3. If I were a shepherd and heard about Jesus, I would rush to find him.

Yes   No   Maybe

4. The shepherds experienced God's presence in their worship together. In which of the following actions do you experience God's presence while you are with your congregation in worship? (Check all that apply.)

• Giving your offering of money
• Saying the Lord's Prayer
• Singing praise songs
• Listening to the Bible read out loud
• Singing traditional hymns
• Listening to a sermon
• Watching a skit or drama presentation
• Listening to announcements
• Hearing the closing prayer
• Watching a movie clip

5. Which people in the story are you most like?

___ I am more like the shepherds who worshiped Christ.
___ I am more like the Bethlehem townspeople who were surprised
   by the story the shepherds told about the angels.

READ OUT LOUD

The Roman Empire was experiencing *Pax Romana*, or Roman Peace, that was brought about by the brutal force of the Roman military. Violently crushing any rebellion on the part of its subjects, Rome ruled supreme. The Roman Empire's few citizens enjoyed this peace while the majority of those living under Roman rule were slaves. Then comes the announcement of the angels (a hymn called "Gloria in Excelsis Deo")—"Glory to God in the highest, and on earth peace to men on whom his favor rests." You can read the story in Luke 2:8-20.

ASK

What adult do you admire most?

DISCUSS, BY THE NUMBERS

1. Use this item to begin a faith conversation about what your group members think surprised the shepherds. Then move your discussion to today—"What surprised you the most when you first heard about Jesus?" "What surprises you the most today about Jesus?"

2. Listen to your group members' responses. Ask, "How is the good news that the shepherds heard the same good news that is told about Jesus today?"

3. See which of the three responses, "Yes, No, or Maybe," were picked the most frequently. Ask, "Why would you rush (or not rush) to find Jesus?" "How much of a rush are you in to find Jesus this Christmas season?"

4. Use this item to prompt a faith conversation about experiencing God's presence in corporate worship. Ask your group to describe what they would do the same and different in worship so that everyone could experience God's presence.

5. Find out who each of your group members see themselves as most like in the story—the shepherds or the townspeople. Share who you are most like. Encourage honesty rather than Sunday school answers. Use this as an opportunity to talk about how both groups of people—the shepherds and the townspeople—experienced God's presence in worship.

CLOSE

Part of worship is experiencing God's presence. We do that together as a congregation and individually throughout the week in our everyday relationship with God. The shepherds experienced God's presence as they worshiped, just like Joseph and Mary, the angels, and probably some of the townspeople.

God is always present in our lives—whether or not we "feel" God close to us. Let us worship God as we become aware of God's presence!

JESUS IS COMING SOON

Getting ready to celebrate Jesus' birth

1. Zechariah learned from the Holy Spirit that Jesus, the Messiah, would arrive soon. Finish this sentence: As Christmas Day gets closer to arriving, I want to…

2. What is one word that best describes how you feel when you think of Jesus' coming at Christmas time?

Hope	Love	Peace
Anticipation	Thankfulness	Forgiveness

3. What do you think—T (true) or F (false)?

___ Christmas reminds us of the people we love.
___ Christmas reminds us that we need more stuff.
___ Christmas reminds us of Jesus' message of forgiveness.
___ Christmas reminds us that we need to find the perfect gifts for those on our list.
___ Christmas reminds us that we don't make enough money.
___ Christmas reminds us we need to decorate.
___ Christmas reminds us we have hope.
___ Christmas reminds us that everyone will go to heaven.
___ Christmas reminds us we should celebrate the birth of Jesus.
___ Christmas reminds us God is alive and working in the world.

4. What is one new thing you can do to get ready to celebrate Christ's birth?

• Perform a secret act of service for one of the members of my family.
• Go without food for a day as I anticipate the arrival of Christ on Christmas Day.
• Read my Bible twice each day in the month of December.
• Set aside 30 minutes to pray one day in December.
• Talk with my family about Jesus every day in December.
• Buy a special gift for my family that demonstrates my love for Christ.
• Pray for others every day.
• Be more grateful.
• Donate things I am no longer using so that someone else can have a better Christmas.
• Share with someone the reason that I celebrate Christmas.

5. Christ came first as a baby, which we celebrate at Christmas. Christ is coming again. When you think about Christ's second coming, what one word best describes how you feel?

Sad   Worried   Scared   Uncertain   Excited   Apathetic   Other _____

READ OUT LOUD

The father of John the Baptizer was none other than Zechariah, the hero in today's story. Zechariah was a Jewish priest at the time of Christ's birth. He was visited by the angel Gabriel and told of the coming birth of his son John (called John the Baptist or John the Baptizer). Because Zechariah didn't believe Gabriel, he was unable to speak until his son's birth. At the birth of John the Baptizer, Zechariah predicted the coming birth of Jesus. This prophecy—in the form of a hymn called the "Benedictus"—prepares us to celebrate Christ's birth. Read the prophecy found in Luke 1:67-75.

ASK

How long does it take you to get ready for school in the morning?

DISCUSS, BY THE NUMBERS

1. Use this item to start a faith conversation about getting ready to celebrate the birth of Jesus. Listen to the group's responses to the sentence stem. Talk about the need to get our hearts and minds ready for the celebration of Christ's birth.

2. See if there were one or two words that were identified the most. Ask your group to identify the reasons behind each of the feeling words.

3. See commentary in bold after each statement.
   - Christmas reminds us of the people we love. **Christmas is a time for good family memories for some and memories of pain for others. Let group members who have painful memories share them in a safe way.**
   - Christmas reminds us that we need more stuff. **Debate this one. Look at the pros and cons of focusing on "stuff" during the Christmas season. Ask, "What would Christmas be like if we bypassed gift-giving and focused exclusively on the birth of Christ through prayer, fasting, Bible reading, worship, and other spiritual disciplines?"**
   - Christmas reminds us of Jesus' message of forgiveness. **Again, debate this one. Ultimately, Christ and the salvation he brings to us is the reason for the season.**
   - Christmas reminds us that we need to find the perfect gifts for those on our list. **Debate this one.**

- Christmas reminds us that we don't make enough money. **Sadly, for many, Christmas is a time of getting into debt or thinking that the size of the gift is the reason for the season.**
- Christmas reminds us we need to decorate. **There is nothing wrong with decorating unless it takes away from the message of Christ at Christmas.**
- Christmas reminds us to have hope. **Ask, "How often do we reflect on the hope we have in Christ?"**
- Christmas reminds us that everyone will go to heaven. **Will everyone go to heaven? The Bible is clear that only those who repent and believe in Jesus are saved.**
- Christmas reminds us we should celebrate the birth of Jesus. **For some it does while for many it reminds them of parties, time off work, and buying gifts they can't afford.**
- Christmas reminds us God is alive and working in the world. **Christmas is a great reminder of what God did over 2,000 years ago and what he is doing now!**

4. What were the five most popular ideas checked by your group members? Talk about other ideas your group may have for getting ready to celebrate Christ's birth.

5. Figure out which one or two words were chosen most. Talk about how we ought to live because Christ is coming again. Read and discuss 2 Peter 3:10-11.

But the day of the Lord will come like a thief. The heavens will disappear with a roar, the elements will be destroyed by fire, and the earth and everything in it will be laid bare. Since everything will be destroyed in this way, what kind of people ought you to be? You ought to live holy and godly lives. (2 Peter 3:10-11)

CLOSE

As Christmas quickly approaches we need to be reminded of the words of Zechariah's song. God rescued us in Jesus Christ. God provided the way of salvation so that we can serve him.

Read Luke 1:74-75. "To rescue us from the hand of our enemies, and to enable us to serve him without fear in holiness and righteousness before him all our days."

THE WISE MEN LOOK FOR JESUS

Everyone is seeking something

1. How many people are searching for a relationship with Jesus?

❏ More than there were in the past
❏ About the same as there were in the past
❏ Fewer than there were in the past

2. If I saw the wise men following the star, I would have—

❏ Joined them
❏ Wondered what they were doing, then forgot about them
❏ Made fun of them
❏ Hid in a cave
❏ Gone ahead of them

3. The star led the wise men to Bethlehem. What or who leads you the most? (Check only one.)

❏ A teacher at school
❏ My friends
❏ My pastor's sermons
❏ Parents/grandparents
❏ My music
❏ Jesus
❏ Extended family
❏ Achievement (in class, in sports)

❏ Advertising
❏ An adult at my church
❏ Video games
❏ The Bible
❏ The opposite sex
❏ Alcohol/drugs
❏ My appearance

4. People are distracted more today from seeking Christ than they were in Jesus' time.

True   False

5. Do you consider yourself a follower of Christ?

❏ Yes   ❏ No

6. What do you want to get out of being a follower of Christ?

❏ A good feeling
❏ Answers to all my prayers
❏ Forgiveness of my sins
❏ A best friend
❏ A ticket into heaven

READ OUT LOUD

The wise men—the Bible never says how many—were educated men from what is now the area of Saudi Arabia, Iraq, and Iran. They were schooled in astronomy, philosophy, religion, and medicine. And they were searching for Jesus. Read the story found in Matthew 2:1-12.

ASK

When you get home from school, what is the first thing you look for?

DISCUSS, BY THE NUMBERS

1. In the United States church attendance has declined. The United States appears to be taking the road Great Britain and Europe have taken by becoming more and more secular. While church attendance is not the only indicator of interest in Jesus, it is the best data we have and probably does indicate less interest in Jesus in the United States. Central and South America, Africa, and parts of Asia are showing much more interest in Jesus and Christianity.

2. Ask, "What do you think the wise men were seeking?" "What do you think Herod was seeking?"

3. Take this opportunity to discuss those things that lead us in good and bad directions. Ask, "Which of these things can lead you astray?" "Which will lead you to Jesus?"

4. People are distracted by all kinds of things—false religions, seeking pleasure, striving to make more money.

5. Talk for a minute about what it means to be a follower of Christ. Ask, "Do you think the wise men became Christ-followers?" Spend time talking with your group about how the forgiveness we have in Christ rights our relationship with God so that we can be friends with God.

6. What do you want to get out of being a follower of Christ?
   - ❏ A good feeling—you can get a good feeling by exercising, eating a great dessert, or going on a fun vacation; you don't need Jesus for a great feeling.
   - ❏ Answers to all my prayers—following Jesus doesn't mean you will get all that you pray for.
   - ❏ Forgiveness of my sins—following Christ does give you this, something you can't get anywhere else.
   - ❏ A best friend—Jesus is the best friend you will ever have.
   - ❏ A ticket into heaven—following Christ will get you into heaven, but this can't be the reason we follow him. We should follow Christ because he is the way, the truth, and the life—there is nowhere else for us to turn.

CLOSE

No matter your social status, your family background, or your education, everyone is seeking something. Some seek pleasure, others power or spiritual enlightenment. The Bible clearly points to Jesus as the only one who will satisfy the spiritual vacuum that exists in our souls.

JOHN THE BAPTIZER PREPARES THE WAY

God wants us to introduce others to Jesus

1. Who first told you about Jesus?

- ❏ A parent or grandparent
- ❏ A friend
- ❏ A neighbor
- ❏ A Sunday school teacher
- ❏ A pastor
- ❏ A book
- ❏ Who's Jesus?
- ❏ Other: _____

2. Are you more like John the Baptizer or the crowds listening to him?

- ❏ John the Baptizer introducing others to Jesus
- ❏ The crowd who listened

3. Why do you think so many people were attracted to John the Baptizer?

- ❏ He acted differently than all the religious people they knew.
- ❏ He wore stylish clothes.
- ❏ He promised them riches if they turned to God.
- ❏ He told them the truth about God.
- ❏ He gave them a purpose for living.
- ❏ He had a weight-loss plan that worked.
- ❏ He pointed them to Jesus.

4. Which one would you choose? If someone asked me about Jesus I would—

a) Change the subject
b) Walk away
c) Tell them to go talk to a pastor
d) Tell them what Jesus has done for me

5. "I tried the church thing once," said Bethany. "My mom made me go to Sunday school after she and my dad got divorced. The kids seemed pretty stuck up. No one talked to me, so I finally stopped going. Why do you want to know?"

Alyssa and Bethany really didn't know each other very well. Bethany just moved to town. Alyssa knew that it was hard to be the new kid, so she had started talking to Bethany during lunch. They mostly just asked each other questions about their favorite movies, kinds of chocolate, and subjects in school. But the last question had stopped the conversation cold. Alyssa had asked Bethany if she and her mom had found a church to go to yet. Now Bethany wanted to know why Alyssa wanted to know. What should Alyssa say?

*In many different ways John preached
the good news to the people. (Luke 3:18, CEV)*

READ OUT LOUD

John the Baptist (or Baptizer, as some have called him) was Jesus' cousin. The Old Testament predicted that John would come before Jesus to get people ready for Jesus' ministry. Read about John the Baptizer from Luke 3:1-20.

ASK

To what famous person would you like to be introduced?

DISCUSS, BY THE NUMBERS

1. The person identified by each of your group members is like John the Baptizer to them. Ask, "How did you respond to that person introducing you to Jesus?"

2. As with most groups, your members will say they are more like the crowds listening to John. Ask, "Why do you think God wants us to introduce others to Jesus as John the Baptizer did?"

3. Discuss the important things that John did to introduce people to Christ.
   - ❏ He acted differently than all the religious people they knew.
   - ❏ He told them the truth about God.
   - ❏ He gave them a purpose for living.
   - ❏ He pointed them to Jesus.

4. Get a faith conversation going about your group's readiness to give an answer to questions about Jesus.

5. Luke 3:18 tells us that John the Baptizer shared the good news of Christ's love and forgiveness in many different ways. There are great and not-so-great ways to tell others about Jesus. This is an ideal situation to discuss effective ways to tell others about Jesus. Let your group identify the top three or four strategies that would work to introduce their friends to Jesus.

In many different ways John preached the good news to the people. (Luke 3:18, CEV)

CLOSE

Sharing Christ is all about getting people interested in Jesus. It may mean you pave the way for someone else to talk with them about Jesus. It may mean you talk directly about the gospel with them. It may mean you and your Christian friends, together and over time, introduce someone to Jesus. John the Baptizer did what he was called to do—introduce Jesus to a lost world in pain. We are called to do the same.

1. **Jesus voluntarily came to John to begin his ministry by being set apart for God through the act of baptism. What are you willing to volunteer to do for Christ?**

   ❏ Talk to someone I know about my faith
   ❏ Invite a friend to church
   ❏ Help teach the little kids at my church
   ❏ Read my Bible once a day
   ❏ Listen to Christian music
   ❏ Ask my parents about their faith
   ❏ Talk to the pastor about a Bible passage
      that I don't understand
   ❏ Dress differently from my friends
   ❏ Carry my Bible at school
   ❏ Ask someone to stop using God's name as a swear word
   ❏ Other: _____

5. Matthew 3:13-17

JESUS GETS BAPTIZED

Getting going in ministry

2. **When it comes to doing ministry, who are you most like?**

   ❏ One of my parents
   ❏ The church custodian
   ❏ My Sunday school teacher
   ❏ My youth leader
   ❏ One of the helpers in the nursery
   ❏ Someone who sits in the back of a worship service
   ❏ Other: _____

3. **Not everyone is baptized in their church building. Some are baptized in swimming pools or even lakes and rivers. Given a choice, where would you like/have liked to be baptized?**

4. **Marcy has heard a lot lately about doing what God wants you to do with your life. She thinks that it sounds a little scary. What if God wants her to do something besides what she is doing now? She likes hanging with her friends and working hard in school. What if God wants her to do something different? Do you think Marcy is ready to do all that God wants her to do with her life?**

5. **To have a ministry for Jesus, we need to take time to pray. When do you usually like to pray? (Check one or more.)**

   ❏ At night looking at the stars
   ❏ In my room before I go to sleep
   ❏ At school before a test
   ❏ When I have a problem
   ❏ When I wonder what decision to make
   ❏ Before Communion

   ❏ With my family
   ❏ At church
   ❏ Before I invite someone to church
   ❏ When I say thank you to God
   ❏ Before worship

READ OUT LOUD

Ministry. Every Christian has one. John the Baptizer had one. You have one. Maybe you don't know what it is yet. Read about John the Baptizer helping Jesus get started in his ministry. Read Matthew 3:13-17.

ASK

What breakfast food gets you going in the morning?

DISCUSS, BY THE NUMBERS

1. See which of the activities were checked the most and the least. These items get your group started talking about ministry.

2. See which of your group members view themselves as leaders, helpers, or not-doing-a-thing people in ministry. We need more leaders and helpers and fewer not-doing-a-thing people.

3. The purpose of this *TalkSheet* is to talk about ministry rather than the doctrinal distinctions regarding baptism. But this can be a good time to talk about your congregation's or denomination's theological perspective on baptism.

4. Listen to your group members' opinions about Marcy's situation. Talk about what it means to do all God wants us to do without being judgmental of those who are not yet ready to fully commit their lives to service.

5. Luke 3:21 tells us that Jesus prayed while he was being baptized. Prayer is essential for any ministry to be effective. All Christians, no matter how young or old, have ministries because they each have been given a spiritual gift by God. They may not be doing the ministry, but they have one. And for that ministry to be effective, it needs to be grounded in prayer.

CLOSE

John the Baptizer helped Jesus begin his ministry. Each of us has a ministry, whether it is leading or helping. Pray for those who are doing ministry presently. Pray for those who are willing to explore a ministry as they get going!

JESUS GETS BIG-TIME TEMPTED

We can use Scripture to handle the temptations we face in our lives

1. Do you **agree (A)** or **disagree (D)** with the following statements?

___ It wasn't fair that Jesus was tempted.
___ I never give in to temptation.
___ Christians are tempted more than people who aren't Christians.
___ Kids are tempted more than adults.

2. What's your opinion?

Satan's temptations are—

When I am facing temptation, I need to—

I am most tempted when—

3. Do you think the following statements are **T (true)** or **F (false)**?
___ Each time Jesus was tempted by the devil, he quoted Scripture.
___ A Christian needs to know the Bible in order to fight against temptation.
___ The Bible reminds us that not having any fun helps us fight temptation.
___ The Bible reveals the truth, which can help us live our lives for God.
___ God's love for us shows throughout the Scripture.

4. Satan tried to confuse Jesus by misquoting the Bible to him. If you are confused about a Bible passage, whom could you ask for help?

5. Underline one of the following three verses. Read the verse. Decide how this passage of Scripture could help you say no to temptation.

Proverbs 3:5-6 • Ephesians 2:10 • 1 John 2:16

READ OUT LOUD

Jesus was tempted—tempted like you and me. All of us have been tempted in the past and will be tempted again and again in the future. The temptation faced by Christ nearly 2,000 years ago can teach us how best to handle any of the temptations we may face in the future. Read what Christ did in Matthew 4:1-11.

ASK

Do you think you would be tempted less if you studied more?

DISCUSS, BY THE NUMBERS

1. See commentary in bold after each statement.
   - It wasn't fair that Jesus was tempted. **Temptation is a fact of life in a world filled with sin. When Jesus chose to come to this world as a human to offer himself as the plan of salvation from sin, he entered a world of temptation.**
   - I never give in to temptation. **Everyone has given in to numerous temptations. That's why we need Christ's death on the cross—to deal with our sins.**
   - Christians are tempted more than people who aren't Christians. **Not really. Life in this sinful world brings temptation followed by temptation.**
   - Kids are tempted more than adults. **This is a great statement to debate with the group.**

2. Listen to your group members' completed sentences. These sentence stems give you a chance to talk about the difficult temptations they face every day (Satan's temptations are—); what they can do when facing temptations (When I am facing temptation, I need to—); and those vulnerable situations that place them at most risk to be tempted (I am most tempted when—).

3. See commentary in bold after each statement.
   - Each time Jesus was tempted by the devil, he quoted Scripture. **Jesus was tempted three times by Satan, and three times he quoted the Bible.**

   - A Christian needs to know the Bible in order to fight against temptation. **If we want to successfully fight against temptation, we should follow Jesus' example and use Scripture. This means we must know what the Bible says.**
   - The Bible reminds us that not having any fun helps us fight temptation. **No, God wants us to have all kinds of fun. This is why God gave basic rules like the Ten Commandments, so that we are protected from those things that don't give us long-lasting fun.**
   - The Bible reveals the truth, which can help us live our lives for God. **Yes, the Bible gives us the truth, and Jesus is the truth.**
   - God's love for us shows throughout the Scripture. **Yes, which we need to remember when we are tempted.**

4. Twisting Scripture is carried out by cults, atheists trying to put down believers, and even naive Christians who don't know any better. Satan quotes Psalm 91:11 but leaves out the second half of the verse. Jesus reminds him of the whole truth. All of your group members need to know several trustworthy adults that they can approach with their confusion.

5. Use one of the Bible verses to spark a faith conversation about how to say no to temptation. Proverbs 3:5-6 • Ephesians 2:10 • 1 John 2:16

CLOSE

Say yes to Jesus. Say yes to the Bible. Say yes to prayer. And you can say no to temptation.

JESUS TALKS WITH NICODEMUS

Sharing the good news at the right time and place

1. Check the one statement that is most accurate. People who don't believe in Jesus—

- ❏ make fun of John 3:16
- ❏ are clueless about John 3:16
- ❏ think the Bible is filled with fables and myths
- ❏ have never read John 3:16
- ❏ ignore John 3:16

2. Nicodemus, a Pharisee and member of the ruling council, came to Jesus under the cover of darkness because...

- ❏ he was worried about his sun-sensitive skin.
- ❏ he was a vampire and could only come out at night.
- ❏ he was afraid of what people might think of him if he approached Jesus during the day.
- ❏ he was a night person.
- ❏ he was embarrassed to be known as a Christ-follower, so he hid his faith.
- ❏ he wanted one-on-one time with Jesus.
- ❏ he wanted time with Jesus but didn't want to lose his job on the ruling council, which opposed Jesus.

3. What do you think Nicodemus wanted out of his conversation with Jesus?

- ❏ A get-out-of-hell-free card
- ❏ The truth about the meaning and purpose of life
- ❏ To find out how he could trick Jesus into saying something wrong
- ❏ How Jesus did the miracles, so he could do them, too
- ❏ Lessons on how to be a better teacher
- ❏ How to have a right relationship with God
- ❏ How to pray so that God the Father would say yes every time
- ❏ Other: _____

4. As Nicodemus saw God in Jesus (John 3:2), people can see God working in my life.

Yes   No   Maybe So

5. How does one put his trust in Jesus?

READ OUT LOUD

What do you think of when you hear John 3:16? A popular Bible verse? Big banners at football games? Nicodemus? Yes, Nicodemus! He was a religious leader who came to Jesus at night. And he was the recipient of that most famous verse, John 3:16. But you probably never think of him when you see the John 3:16 banners held up by fans during extra-point kicks. Well, now, maybe you will. Read his story in John 3:1-21.

ASK

Have you memorized John 3:16?

DISCUSS, BY THE NUMBERS

1. Here's a great faith conversation starter to get your group talking about sharing the good news found in John 3:16.
2. After talking about Nicodemus' possible fear of being seen with Jesus, ask, "How embarrassed are you to be known as a follower of Christ?"
3. Possible answers could include—
   • A get-out-of-hell-free card
   • The meaning and purpose of life
   • How to have a right relationship with God
   • Love
   • Hope
   • Help for his problems
4. One of the best ways for us to be witnesses is through how we live in front of others. See how your group thinks they are doing.
5. Here is a simple explanation you can use with your group:

   God created us with the freedom to choose to live a self-centered life or to obey God. Since we chose our selfish way of wrongdoing, we are separated from God. No matter what we do—how good we try to be, what self-help books we read, or what religion we try to follow—we can't reach God.

   But God has reached out to us through Jesus Christ. God made a way for us to be forgiven of our self-centered ways. Jesus died on a cross and came back from the grave. His death paid the price for our wrongdoing, our sin, and now we can have a friendship with God and experience the promised new life. So how should we respond to God's offer of Jesus Christ?

God loved the people of this world so much that he gave his only Son, so that everyone who has faith in him will have eternal life and never really die. God did not send his Son into the world to condemn its people. He sent him to save them!
(John 3:16-17, CEV)

You need only to put your trust in Jesus Christ. It's as easy as **A-B-C**. First, you need to **A**dmit that you need Jesus, that you are a sinner separated from God. Second, you need to **B**elieve in Jesus Christ, that he died, came back to life so that your sins could be forgiven, and is your only hope for a relationship with God. Third, **C**ommit your life to Jesus Christ so that he controls your life rather than your selfish desires.

Are you ready for these **ABC**s? Here is a prayer you can pray to get you started:

*Dear Jesus, I **A**dmit that I am a sinner, that I need you. I **B**elieve you died for my sins. I give my sins to you and ask for forgiveness. I **C**ommit my will and my life to you so that you take control. I want to follow you as my Savior and Lord. In Jesus' name I pray. Amen.*

CLOSE

Telling others about the good news is as easy as **A-B-C**. So let's review. First, you need to **A**dmit that you need Jesus, that you are a sinner separated from God. Second, you need to **B**elieve in Jesus Christ, that he died, came back to life so that your sins could be forgiven, and is your only hope for a relationship with God. Third, **C**ommit your life to Jesus Christ so that he controls your life rather than your selfish desires.

THE WOMAN AT THE WELL

Jesus cares about our spiritual emptiness

1. **Jesus used his thirst as an opportunity to start a faith conversation with the woman at the well. Rank the following strategies for starting a faith conversation with those you know who don't believe in Jesus from great (1) to not-so-great (7).**

___ Preach at them and include the word *hell* in your preaching

___ Ask them what they think of Jesus

___ Invite them to your church

___ Wait for them to ask you about Jesus

___ Ask them if they need you to pray about something in their lives

___ Talk about Jesus when the conversation turns to spiritual issues

___ Use a practical situation to talk about Jesus

2. **What do you think? Y=Yes, N=No, or MS=Maybe So**

___ My friends are spiritually ignorant.

___ My friends don't know the meaning of grace.

___ My friends don't want anything to do with Jesus.

___ My friends are interested in spiritual things.

___ My friends listen when I talk about Jesus.

3. **What do you think? People who haven't experienced God's love and forgiveness—**

❏ are missing out.   ❏ will do just fine.

4. **The woman at the well needed to see the emptiness in her life before she was ready to turn to Christ. How could you help your friends who don't know Christ see their spiritual emptiness?**

❏ I don't think I can.

❏ I'm not sure that they are spiritually empty without Christ.

❏ I have no clue what spiritual emptiness means.

❏ I could talk about how empty my life would be without Christ.

5. **Jesus got the woman interested in him with lots of probing questions. What got you interested in Jesus?**

READ OUT LOUD

She was a woman, in biblical times considered a second-class citizen at best. And a Samaritan, hated by the Jews. Jesus talked with her. Cared about her spiritual emptiness. Read the story found in John 4:3-30.

ASK

Who cares about you the most?

DISCUSS, BY THE NUMBERS

1. Have a faith conversation about how to start faith conversations. Look at each of the statements and decide which faith conversation-starting technique is the best.

   - Preach at them and include the word *hell* in your preaching. **This is the opposite of what Christ did with the woman at the well. He didn't preach *at* her but talked *with* her.**

   - Ask them what they think of Jesus. **A good way to get started. Talk about what to do next if they show interest or don't show interest in Christ.**

   - Invite them to your church. **A special event could be a great introduction to Jesus and spark further interest in knowing more about Jesus.**

   - Wait for them to ask you about Jesus. **They may never ask!**

   - Ask them if they need you to pray about something in their lives. **Great idea, especially if there are specific needs in their lives.**

   - Talk about Jesus when the conversation turns to spiritual issues. **Another great idea—especially at those times of the year, like Christmas and Easter, when spiritual things are more often discussed. Also Jewish and Muslim holidays can bring up spiritual issues that can segue into a conversation about Jesus.**

   - Use a practical situation to talk about Jesus. **When a friend talks about a painful situation, for example, it can lead into a faith conversation about the comfort Jesus can give.**

2. Tell a story from your life about your experience with spiritual emptiness and God's grace. Use this story as a springboard to talk about your group members' friends' interest in Jesus.

3. Listen to your group's responses. Ask, "*What are they missing out on?*"

4. Jesus used the emptiness the woman experienced in her marriages to show her that she was spiritually empty. Talk about what it takes before someone is ready to confess sins and turn to Jesus.

5. Talk about what might get your group members' friends interested in Jesus.

CLOSE

Every human being on the planet is spiritually empty without Christ. Religions (and there are many around the world) strive to fill that spiritual emptiness. The religion of atheism explains away the emptiness by saying it doesn't exist. But it does—and the emptiness can only be filled by a relationship with Jesus Christ.

JESUS HEALS A GOVERNMENT OFFICIAL'S SON

You can count on Christ every day of the week

1. **The government official urgently needed Jesus to perform a miracle of healing for his son. How much do you need Jesus?**

   ❏ I need Jesus every day.
   ❏ I often need Jesus.
   ❏ I sometimes need Jesus.
   ❏ I need Jesus once in a while.
   ❏ I don't really need Jesus.

2. **Circle those that are true for you.**

   a) I tend to forget about Jesus when things are going well in my life.
   b) I have an easy time relying on Jesus when I'm really worried.
   c) I feel closest to Jesus when I'm having problems in my life.
   d) I rely more on Jesus when I am praying regularly.
   e) I have a difficult time relying on Jesus when things aren't going well with my friends.

3. **What do you think? It takes a life crisis for people to turn to Jesus.**

   ❏ Always true   ❏ Sometimes true
   ❏ Usually true   ❏ Never true

4. **Do you think Jesus heals people today? Why or why not?**

5. **The government official (and everyone in his home) put his faith in Jesus after he experienced the miracle. What did it take for you to put your faith in Jesus?**

READ OUT LOUD

The people of Galilee—that region of the country where Jesus grew up—saw him perform miracles in Jerusalem during the Passover. Many put their faith in him as the Messiah. When Jesus was returning to Galilee, a government official hurried to him and begged that he come heal his sick son. The man had enough faith to know that Jesus could make his dying son well. Read the story from John 4:45-54.

ASK

What candy bar do you count on to always taste great?

DISCUSS, BY THE NUMBERS

1. See which of the boxes your group members checked. Ask, "What does it mean to need Jesus every day?" "Why do some people think they don't need Jesus at all?"

2. Explore why we so often turn to Jesus when in a crisis but then neglect our relationship with him when things are going well. Ask, "What might happen if you deepened your relationship with Christ during the good times so that when the bad times arrived you could more easily count on Christ?" "Can you name a crisis time that brought you closer to Christ?"

3. Tell a story of someone you know (it could be you) who put his/her faith in Christ as a result of a major life crisis.

4. You can debate the honesty of "faith healers" if you choose. The point here is not that you need a faith healer to pray over you for healing, but that Jesus does heal. Ask, "Have you ever prayed for someone who was healed of cancer or another major illness?"

5. Tell the story of when you put your faith in Christ. Describe what it took for you to put your faith in Jesus.

CLOSE

The government official believed that Jesus could heal his son from the serious illness that was killing him—if only Jesus would come to his home. The man seemed to think that Jesus had to be with his son for the healing to occur. The man had not yet put his faith in Jesus as the Messiah. Jesus stretched the man's faith by healing the boy from a distance. And it was that action that led the man to put his faith in Jesus as his Savior. The man learned that he could count on Jesus whether he was present or far away. And we learn that we too can count on Jesus every day!

JESUS' FAMILY WANTS TO SEE HIM

You can count on Christ every day
of the week

1. Check the following messages that you think are from God.

- ❑ Honesty is the best policy.
- ❑ Love God with all you have.
- ❑ All paths lead to God.
- ❑ As long as no one gets hurt, you can do what you want.
- ❑ Always look out for number one.
- ❑ Get what you can from a friendship and move on.
- ❑ Store up treasures in heaven.
- ❑ Obey your parents.
- ❑ Grab all the fun you can.
- ❑ Treat others the way you want to be treated.

2. How do you hear what Christ has to say? Check all that apply.

- ❑ Ask if your decisions are decisions Jesus would make.
- ❑ Study other religions like Islam and Hinduism.
- ❑ Practice the spiritual discipline of silence, listening for the Holy Spirit.
- ❑ Ask trustworthy Christian friends (peers and adults).
- ❑ Read the Gospels in a red-letter Bible (one in which Christ's words appear in red print).
- ❑ Check your astrological reading in the newspaper.
- ❑ Read a devotional book every day.
- ❑ Pray regularly.
- ❑ Participate in a weekly Bible study.

3. Do you agree or disagree with this statement?

We can be close to Jesus—like we're in his family.   ❑ I agree   ❑ I disagree

4. Which of the following are examples of putting the word of God into practice?

- ❑ Worshiping God with your congregation
- ❑ Reading your Bible
- ❑ Spending an hour each day on Facebook® or MySpace®
- ❑ Doing yard work for your neighbor who just got out of the hospital
- ❑ Putting money in the offering plate
- ❑ Giving your sister a ride to school when your mom can't
- ❑ Listening to music with questionable lyrics
- ❑ Going to a Christian music concert
- ❑ Going on a mission trip this summer
- ❑ Only hanging out with the popular people at church
- ❑ Skipping a meal and donating the money to your church's hunger project

5. How will your life be better or worse because you are obedient to Christ?

READ OUT LOUD

Jesus loved his family, especially his mother. His first miracle was in response to a concern his mother had. And yet he seemed to brush off his family in today's story. Read the story found in Luke 8:19-21.

ASK

How big is your extended family?

DISCUSS, BY THE NUMBERS

1. Each of the checked boxes is a message from God that can be found in the Bible.

   Jesus asserts in today's story that we can be part of his family by hearing and obeying what he tells us. This means we must discern what messages are from Jesus and the Bible and what messages are contrary to Jesus' teaching.
   - ✔ Honesty is the best policy.
   - ✔ Love God with all you have.
   - ❑ All paths lead to God. **Contrary to biblical teaching.**
   - ❑ As long as no one gets hurt, you can do what you want. **Contrary to biblical teaching.**
   - ❑ Always look out for number one. **Contrary to biblical teaching.**
   - ❑ Get what you can from a friendship and move on. **Contrary to biblical teaching.**
   - ✔ Store up treasures in heaven.
   - ✔ Obey your parents.
   - ❑ Grab all the fun you can. **If the fun you seek is sinful (or more important to you than pleasing God), then it's wrong.**
   - ✔ Treat others the way you want to be treated.

2. All of the checked statements are ways your group members can hear Christ.
   - ❑ Ask if your decisions are decisions Jesus would make.
   - ❑ Study other religions like Islam and Hinduism.
   - ✔ Practice the spiritual discipline of silence, listening for the Holy Spirit.
   - ✔ Ask trustworthy Christian friends (peers and adults).
   - ✔ Read the Gospels in a red-letter Bible (in which Christ's words appear in red print).

   - ❑ Check your astrological reading in the newspaper.
   - ✔ Read a devotional book every day.
   - ✔ Pray regularly.
   - ✔ Participate in a weekly Bible study.

3. While Jesus clearly loved his earthly family, this passage reveals that he views obedience to God as a sign that you're in his family, just as if you were a blood relative.

4. Each of the checked statements speaks to hearing and obeying God. Talk about how you and your group members can make each of the statements true in your lives.
   - ✔ Worshiping God with your congregation
   - ✔ Reading your Bible
   - ❑ Spending an hour each day on Facebook® or MySpace®
   - ✔ Doing yard work for your neighbor who just got out of the hospital
   - ✔ Putting money in the offering plate
   - ❑ Listening to music with questionable lyrics
   - ✔ Going to a Christian music concert
   - ✔ Going on a mission trip this summer
   - ❑ Only hanging out with the popular people at church
   - ✔ Skipping a meal and donating the money to your church's hunger project

5. Life is obviously better when we obey Christ. "Life is better" doesn't mean you won't suffer, face loss, or hurt (just like people who don't follow Christ). But you will have Christ with you as you go through the tough times in life, and you will have eternal life.

CLOSE

Though Jesus seemed to brush his family aside, that was not the case. A look at his life shows that he loved them. Jesus used an interruption by his mom and brothers to teach the crowd a life lesson. Read Luke 8:21. Jesus invites everyone to follow him and to be part of his family by hearing and obeying what he says.

"My mother and brothers are those who hear God's word and put it into practice."
Jesus, in Luke 8:21

"WHO DO YOU SAY I AM?"

Who is Jesus to you?

1. If you were to take a survey of people at the mall, who would they say Jesus is?

❏ Jesus never existed.
❏ Jesus was a moral leader.
❏ Jesus was a prophet sent from God.
❏ Jesus is my Lord and Savior, the Son of God.
❏ Jesus was a lunatic.
❏ Jesus was an angel.
❏ I don't know and I don't care.

2. If someone were to ask you who Jesus is, what would you tell them? Check all that apply.

❏ I don't know who he is.
❏ He is God.
❏ He is one of many ways to heaven.
❏ He died and came back to life for the forgiveness of their sins.
❏ He is my Savior.
❏ He is someone you don't talk about.

3. To me, Jesus is—

❏ Lord of every aspect of my life
❏ Lord of most parts of my life
❏ Lord of some parts of my life
❏ Lord of a little bit of my life
❏ Not Lord of my life

4. What do you think—yes or no?

Can you accept the forgiveness offered by Christ? **Y / N**

Can you tell others about the love Jesus has for them? **Y / N**

Can you let Christ give you the freedom from sin you need? **Y / N**

5. Why do you think Jesus didn't want the crowds to know his true identity until after his death and resurrection?

❏ The paparazzi would be everywhere.
❏ The crowds didn't yet know enough about Jesus.
❏ Jesus was in the Israeli witness protection program.
❏ Jesus didn't want his timetable to be disturbed.
❏ Jesus didn't want to be seen as a political revolutionary.
❏ Jesus had reached his miracle quota for the year.
❏ The resurrection would be the proof that people needed to believe in Jesus as Savior and Lord.
❏ Jesus didn't want to be hounded by autograph seekers.

READ OUT LOUD

After the feeding of 5,000-plus people, Jesus goes off for some alone time with the disciples and to pray. While away from the crowds, he asks his disciples the most important question of all time. Read the short story from Luke 9:18-22.

ASK

If you pretended to be someone else, would people be able to guess who you were?

DISCUSS, BY THE NUMBERS

1. See how many of your group members believe mallgoers would say, "Jesus is my Lord and Savior, the Son of God," or something to that effect.

2. The checked boxes are orthodox Christian beliefs.
   - ❏ I don't know who he is.
   - ✔ He is God.
   - ❏ He is one of many ways to heaven.
   - ✔ He died and came back to life for the forgiveness of their sins.
   - ✔ He is my Savior.
   - ❏ He is someone you don't talk about.

3. Jesus has a claim on our lives. He wants to be in total control—Lord of every aspect of our lives. Ask, "What helps us make Jesus Lord of every aspect of our lives?"

4. Though each of the three questions is a yes-no question, they can spark all kinds of faith conversations. Feel free to have one now.

5. See commentary in bold after the checked statements.
   - ❏ The paparazzi would be everywhere.
   - ✔ The crowds didn't yet know enough about Jesus. **Yes. They needed Jesus to teach them more.**
   - ❏ Jesus was in the Israeli witness protection program.
   - ✔ Jesus didn't want his timetable to be disturbed. **Yes. If the people knew, then their reactions would interfere with God's plans.**
   - ❏ Jesus didn't want to be seen as a political revolutionary.
   - ❏ Jesus had reached his miracle quota for the year.
   - ✔ The resurrection would be the proof that people needed to believe in Jesus as Savior and Lord. **Yes. Once the word got out about Jesus' resurrection, many put their faith in Christ.**
   - ❏ Jesus didn't want to be hounded by autograph seekers.

CLOSE

The disciples told Jesus that the crowds who listened to his teaching believed Jesus was someone important, like a prophet. So Jesus, in Luke 9:20, asked the disciples, *"Who do you say I am?"* Peter—the unofficial spokesman for the disciples—said, "The Christ of God." Jesus is still asking that very same question of us today—"Who do you say I am?"

1. I live to follow Christ—

- ❑ On Sunday mornings
- ❑ Every day
- ❑ Most days
- ❑ When I remember to
- ❑ When my mom reminds me to
- ❑ When I feel ashamed of my sins

2. Circle the one phrase that best describes indulging yourself.

Thinking only of me	Putting me first
I'm the center of the Universe	It's all about me
Me first, me second, me third	I'm just too good to be true

3. Choosing to follow Jesus—

- ❑ Happens every day of my life
- ❑ Happens when I need him
- ❑ Happens when I feel guilty
- ❑ Happens sometimes
- ❑ Should happen more often
- ❑ Doesn't happen in my life

4. Jesus says that you must make a conscious effort to "take up your cross daily" as you follow him.

- ❑ All of the Christians I know do this.
- ❑ Most of the Christians I know do this.
- ❑ Some of the Christians I know do this.
- ❑ None of the Christians I know do this.

5. Underline the top three ways you could give up your life in order to save it.

Show kindness to others	Talk with others about Christ's love
Do anything I want	Criticize others
Recycle	Do what I think is best
Ignore my chores	Carry in groceries for an older neighbor
Smile at the new kid at school	Blow off studying for a test and play video games

6. Place an X on the line below, indicating what you think will happen to you because you are a Christ-follower.

◆○○○○○○○◆○○○○○○○◆○○○○○○○◆○○○○○○○◆○○○○○○○◆
RIDICULED   CONSIDERED COOL

READ OUT LOUD

Jesus is about to teach his followers something hard to understand. But first Jesus tells the disciples he will soon pay the biggest price he can for their salvation—Jesus will die for them. Then Jesus teaches his followers what it will cost to follow him. Read the story found in Luke 9:22-26.

ASK

What does it cost you to get a college degree?

DISCUSS, BY THE NUMBERS

1. Encourage honesty, not the Sunday school answer. Talk about what it means to follow Christ every day versus following the ways of this world.
2. See if your group can together choose one phrase that best describes indulging yourself—the opposite of denying yourself.
3. Talk about the daily choice we have to deny ourselves and give Christ control or take control back from Christ and live the way we want.
4. Ask, "Why daily?" Answer: This is not a salvation passage but a discipleship passage. This is a daily decision to make Christ the Lord of every aspect and corner of our lives. Let your group members know that many Christians make Jesus their Savior but not their Lord. They aren't taking up their cross daily. We call this hypocrisy.
5. The checked statements are examples of losing your life while the unchecked are examples of trying to gain the world.
   - ✔ Show kindness to others
   - ✔ Talk with others about Christ's love
   - ❑ Do anything I want
   - ❑ Criticize others
   - ✔ Recycle
   - ❑ Do what I think is best
   - ❑ Ignore my chores
   - ✔ Carry in groceries for an older neighbor
   - ✔ Smile at the new kid at school
   - ❑ Blow off studying for a test and play video games
6. Use the line scale to talk about Luke 9:26. Likely all Christians are made fun of at some point in their lives because of their relationship with Jesus Christ. Ask, "Does it matter if you're made fun of because you follow Jesus?"

"If anyone is ashamed of me and my words, the Son of Man will be ashamed of him when he comes in his glory and in the glory of the Father and of the holy angels."—Jesus, in Luke 9:26

CLOSE

Condemned criminals carried the crossbeam to the place where they would be crucified. We are like those criminals in that we should die for our sins. But because we place our faith in Jesus, we are then "crucified with Christ"—as if we endured Christ's sacrifice, even though he did it alone—and we belong to him. So Jesus now asks us to forget about ourselves and live a life of sacrifice. So we denounce ourselves and our sin and walk with Jesus in sacrificial love.

DISCOUNTING JESUS

Finding a way around what Jesus tells us

1. How do you think Jesus preached the gospel about himself?

- ❑ He yelled and screamed.
- ❑ He asked for money.
- ❑ He told the people to turn from their sins, put their trust in him, and follow him.
- ❑ He zapped people with lightning if they didn't believe.
- ❑ He told stories about the kingdom of God.
- ❑ He showed compassion to the people as he talked.
- ❑ He played the organ while he preached.

2. Which of these statements do you think is the most true?

- ❑ The religious leaders wanted the best for Jesus.
- ❑ Jesus was right, and the religious leaders were wrong.
- ❑ The religious leaders wanted Jesus dead.
- ❑ Jesus was just like the religious leaders.
- ❑ Jesus knew the religious leaders were deceiving the people.
- ❑ Belief in Jesus by the people was eroding the power of the religious leaders.

3. Who are your friends most like?

- ❑ The people who believed in Jesus as the Messiah.
- ❑ The religious leaders who knew what Jesus said but refused to believe.
- ❑ People who have no idea what Jesus said.

4. Do you think that each of these statements is T (true) or F (false)?

___ Being a Christian is much easier than being a non-Christian.
___ People twist what Jesus said so they can keep sinning.
___ Not everything the Bible says about Jesus can be true.
___ The Bible recorded everything that Jesus said.
___ Jesus said some controversial things.

5. What do you think of Kiara's attitude?

"I don't like her," Kiara said to her friend Juanita as she stared at the girl who walked into the room.

"You mean Mandy?" Juanita asked. "Why?"

"Because she doesn't like me," said Kiara. "I can't like anybody who doesn't like me back."

READ OUT LOUD

The religious leaders were trying to discredit what Jesus had to say. Jesus was teaching the day after he cleaned out the money-hungry vendors in the temple. Read the story found in Luke 20:1-26.

ASK

What chore do you try hardest to avoid?

DISCUSS, BY THE NUMBERS

1. Did he yell and scream? Ask for lots of money? Play the organ? Jesus did the following three things (and more).
   ✔ He told the people to turn from their sins, put their trust in him, and follow him.
   ✔ He told stories about the kingdom of God.
   ✔ He showed compassion to the people as he talked.

2. See commentary in bold after each statement.
   ❑ The religious leaders wanted the best for Jesus. **No, they wanted Jesus out of the way.**
   ❑ Jesus was right and the religious leaders were wrong. **Yes, and they didn't want to be wrong.**
   ❑ The religious leaders wanted Jesus dead. **Yes, they were looking for ways to end his life.**
   ❑ Jesus was just like the religious leaders. **Jesus was just the opposite.**
   ❑ Jesus knew the religious leaders were deceiving the people. **Yes, and he told them so on several occasions.**
   ❑ Belief in Jesus by the people was eroding the power of the religious leaders. **Yes, because so many people were putting their faith in Christ.**

3. See which statements your group members picked and then discuss what this means to their relationship with their friends.

4. See commentary in bold after each statement.
   • Being a Christian is much easier than being a non-Christian. **A good one to discuss. Some may say it's the opposite—but is it, really? It may be fun to live with no God to obey or please—but for how long? And at what cost?**
   • People twist what Jesus said so they can keep sinning. **This is often the case. People want to rationalize and justify their actions.**
   • Not everything the Bible says about Jesus can be true. **If some of it is not true, then you must conclude that none of it is true.**
   • The Bible recorded everything that Jesus said. **No. Nor did it record everything he did.**
   • Jesus said some controversial things. **Yes. And those things got him crucified.**

5. Ask, "How did Kiara justify her attitude?" "How do we often justify our behavior to get around what Jesus said in Scripture?"

CLOSE

Why do we try, like the religious leaders in Jesus' time, to find a way around what Jesus tells us? Because we don't like what he said, or we don't want to do what he wants us to do. Yet, if we want to follow Jesus, we must stop looking for the loopholes and start living like him.

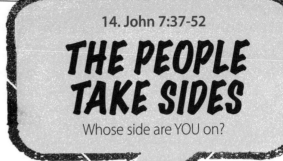

THE PEOPLE TAKE SIDES

Whose side are YOU on?

1. Why do you think the Pharisees were so annoyed by Jesus? (Check all the statements that apply.)

• Jesus was a threat to their jobs.
• Jesus was better looking.
• Jesus knew the Old Testament better than the Pharisees.
• Jesus could get into the better restaurants.
• Jesus was popular with many of the people.
• Jesus spoke the truth.
• Jesus was a better dresser.

2. What do you think impressed the temple soldiers the most about Jesus? (Check all the statements that apply.)

• They would have been exposed to many teachers in the temple, and Jesus stood out.
• Jesus bribed the temple soldiers so that they would say good stuff about him.
• They recognized something different about Jesus.
• Jesus let them borrow his big-screen TV.
• The temple soldiers were peer-pressured by the crowd.
• They had never heard anyone teach the truth as Jesus had.
• They knew a good opinion of Jesus would make their bosses, the Pharisees, really mad.

3. What do you think? Jesus was controversial in his day because—

4. What do you think?

	DEFINITELY	SOMETIMES	NOPE
a) To follow Christ means to stay away from nonbelievers.	❑	❑	❑
b) To follow Christ means to give up money.	❑	❑	❑
c) To follow Christ means you must suffer.	❑	❑	❑
d) To follow Christ means you will experience unbelievable joy.	❑	❑	❑
e) To follow Christ means you can't play violent video games.	❑	❑	❑

5. Whose side are you on? (Check only one answer.)

• Committed to following the ways of the world
• Wanting to follow Christ but following the ways of the world
• Trying to follow Christ
• Committed to following Christ

READ OUT LOUD

Because Jesus stood to preach in the middle of a ceremony in which the priest drew water from the Siloam Pool, Jesus' words of spiritual thirst and living water would have had special significance to those in attendance at this religious ceremony. In fact, it was so significant that his message divided the large crowd. Read the story found in John 7:37-52.

ASK

Whose side are you usually on when you play a game—the winning or losing side?

DISCUSS, BY THE NUMBERS

1. Identify which of the statements was most popular with your group. Discuss why your group members think Jesus was so popular with the people of the day. Ask, "Do these same reasons hold true today?"

2. Find out which of the statements was checked the most by your group. Start a faith conversation around the following three statements.
   ✔ They would have been exposed to many teachers in the temple, and Jesus stood out.
   ✔ They recognized something different about Jesus.
   ✔ They had never heard anyone teach the truth as Jesus had.

3. The people in the story debated Jesus' identity. Some were convinced that he was the long-awaited Savior. Others thought he was some sort of prophet. The Pharisees wanted to get rid of him altogether. People today also have varying opinions as to who Jesus really was (and is). Who do people say Jesus is today? There is enough evidence to prove that Jesus Christ did, in fact, exist. We are left to decide if he is God, as he said; a liar; or a lunatic. Ask your group to draw some conclusions about what people today think about Jesus.

4. See commentary in bold next to each of the statements.
   a) To follow Christ means to stay away from non-believers. **Sometimes, yes, you need to stay away from certain people who are a bad influence. Yet, we should have friends who don't follow Christ, so we can share the gospel with them in the natural course of the relationship, love them as our neighbors, and help transform our culture for Christ.**
   b) To follow Christ means to give up money. **Not at all. Money is neutral—neither good nor bad. It's what you do with money as a Christ-follower that matters.**
   c) To follow Christ means you must suffer. **You will suffer at times for following Christ. And some of us will suffer more than others (see 1 Peter 2:21).**
   d) To follow Christ means you will experience unbelievable joy. **Definitely! (Galatians 5:22)**
   e) To follow Christ means you can't play violent video games. **Debate this one!**

5. Get an honest faith conversation going about "taking sides"—following the world or following Christ.

CLOSE

Read John 7:43 to your group. Say, "Jesus has been causing divisions for the past 2,000 years. As followers of Jesus we struggle with how to live in the world without letting the world live in us. There are no easy answers or simple steps we can take to successfully follow Christ 100 percent of the time. But we do know that Jesus walks with us as we submit our lives to him one day at a time."

The people started taking sides against each other because of Jesus. (John 7:43, CEV)

NOT A GUESSING GAME

Jesus is who he said he is

1. **People at the holiday celebration wanted to know who Jesus was. People at my school or on my sports team also want to know who Jesus is.**

   For Sure   Sometimes   Not Really

2. **How old were you when you first heard about Jesus?**

   • Too young to remember
   • Four or five
   • Elementary school
   • Middle school

3. **What are the possible roadblocks that keep people from putting their faith in Christ?**

   • They don't know how.
   • They want to be in charge of their own lives.
   • They think their good works will be all it takes to get them into heaven.
   • They don't want to give up their immoral lifestyles.
   • They think Jesus is for weak people.
   • They just don't think about it.
   • They have never heard of Jesus.

4. **Check the box after each statement that best describes you.**

	ALWAYS	MOSTLY	SOMETIMES	NEVER
• I live like Jesus is Lord of my life.	☐	☐	☐	☐
• The Bible has authority over my life.	☐	☐	☐	☐
• I regularly pray for Christ's guidance.	☐	☐	☐	☐
• I know that Jesus is coming again.	☐	☐	☐	☐
• I talk often to others about what Jesus has done for me.	☐	☐	☐	☐

5. **Claudisa really wanted to go to the movie with her friend Abby, but it was on Wednesday night and she really didn't want to miss youth group that night.**

   "Well," said Abby, "can you come or not?"

   "I would really like to," said Claudisa, "but I can't because youth group is on that night."

   "Why do you make such a big deal about this Jesus thing?" Abby asked.

   What would you say if you were Claudisa?

READ OUT LOUD

Today's story occurred during the Feast of Dedication or Lights (called Hanukkah today). This winter holiday commemorated Israel's rescue from an oppressive Roman emperor, Antiochus Epiphanes, by the Jewish leader, Judas Maccabeus. Once again, the Jewish people were facing oppression by the Roman Empire. So on the minds of many Jewish people that day was the identification of the long-awaited Messiah. Who was he? How would he deliver them from the oppression they now faced? Read the story found in John 10:22-42.

ASK

What identification do you have that shows you are who you say you are?

DISCUSS, BY THE NUMBERS

1. Tally the responses of your group members. Ask, "How are the people at your school or on your sports team like the Jews at the holiday celebration?" "How are they different?"

2. This item takes the discussion about Jesus from friends to the personal. Identify the different ages when your group members first heard of Jesus. Tell the group that the reason the Jews wanted to stone Jesus was because he said he was God. The crime of blasphemy was death by stoning. Either Jesus is God, as he said, or he deserved to be stoned to death. That is the decision before your group today—is Jesus who he said he is?

3. See commentary in bold after each statement: What are the possible roadblocks that keep people from putting their faith in Christ?

   - They don't know how. **Get a good faith conversation going on this one. Is this true or an excuse?**
   - They want to be in charge of their own lives. **To declare that Jesus is God means that he has a claim on our lives. And that means we can't run our lives the way we want to run them.**
   - They think their good works will be all it takes to get them into heaven. **Good works as the way to heaven fool many, many people. We want to believe that we can be good enough to please God. It's offensive to think that there is nothing**
   we can do to gain God's acceptance. Yet, we must accept by faith God's gift of Jesus for his acceptance of us.
   - They don't want to give up their immoral lifestyles. **Yes, there are many who want to live on their own terms rather than submit to God.**
   - They think Jesus is for weak people. **Jesus said that he came for the sick, not the healthy (see Matthew 9:12). By that Jesus meant he came for those who know they are broken and need a Savior rather than those who believe they can live on their own. So yes, Jesus did come for the weak. The reality is—we are all weak, but some of us don't want to admit it.**
   - They just don't think about it. **Many people are so busy with the day-to-day pursuit of life that they push God, heaven, spiritual matters, and Jesus out of their consciousness. It takes work, but some manage to "just not think about Jesus."**
   - They have never heard of Jesus. **Sadly, many people around the world, especially in countries with large Muslim populations, have never heard of Jesus.**

4. Today's story looked at the unbelief of some of the Jews. The purpose of this activity is to allow your group members to affirm their faith in Christ.

5. Talk about the pros and cons of the different responses.

Note: When Jesus replied to the Jews about them being "gods," he was referring to Psalm 82:6. Here Jesus was saying that the word *god* means a leader chosen by God for a certain task. Jesus then goes on to imply that he's God's son, chosen by God the Father for a specific task. Jesus was not saying that they are, or would become, a "god." That is a gross misinterpretation of Scripture.

CLOSE

Remember, Jesus told the Jewish leaders that he is God. Here's the question before us today: Is Jesus who he said he is? The answer to that question makes all the difference in the world. It shapes our very lives, guides all our decisions, and greatly influences how we think and act on a daily basis!

THE STORY OF THE GOOD SAMARITAN

Who is your neighbor?

1. The lawyer wanted to show Jesus that he knew what he was talking about. He was looking to justify his behavior and prove to Jesus that he had kept the law and deserved a place in heaven. How often do your friends try to say their inappropriate behavior is okay? How about you?

2. Through his questions Jesus was leading the lawyer to an understanding of his own sinfulness—that he wasn't able to keep the law and needed a Savior. On the line scale below, place an X where you see yourself.

How aware are you of your brokenness?

| 1 | 2 | 3 | 4 | 5 |

CLUELESS   TOTALLY AWARE

3. It would be expected that either the priest or the Levite would have helped the beaten man, a fellow Israelite. Why do you think Jesus had them avoid their countryman in need of help? (Circle the one answer you think is most likely.)

   • This might have been a common occurrence.
   • To show that, because they didn't know the person, they didn't feel obligated to see him as their neighbor.
   • One would have to take a risk to help the victim of the robbery.
   • It would cost them money to help the beaten man.
   • Jesus wanted to show that most people have a narrow definition of who their neighbor is.

4. Do you A (agree) or D (disagree) with each of these statements?

   ___ No one today acts like the Samaritan.
   ___ The victim was just asking to be robbed by traveling alone; he didn't deserve help.
   ___ There's no reward in being a good Samaritan.
   ___ I am more like the Samaritan than the priest or Levite.

5. Donnette was so angry. Sara, the girl who sits next to her in Algebra, cheated off her and got caught. Not only did Sara get her paper taken away, but so did Donnette! Donnette sees Sara crying in the hall. She knows that Sara will probably flunk the class now. What should Donnette say to Sara?

6. Jesus asked the lawyer to identify the neighbor in the story. Who is your neighbor?

READ OUT LOUD

Jesus used the story of the Good Samaritan to make a point. Jesus was teaching us about our neighbor—specifically about who our neighbor is. To really understand this story, we need a little background first.

A priest at the time was a person from the tribe of Levi whose job was to offer sacrifices to God for the sins of the people. A Levite, again from the tribe of Levi, assisted the priest in temple duties. A Samaritan was considered a half-breed with foreign blood, hated, and not worthy of any Jewish person's attention. Now you are ready for the story. Read it in Luke 10:25-37.

ASK

How well do you know the people who live next door to you?

DISCUSS, BY THE NUMBERS

1. The lawyer thought he was keeping the Ten Commandments and, therefore, would get eternal life in heaven. He asked questions to trick Jesus into saying something wrong. Talk about the "whys" of justifying our inappropriate behavior.

2. After your group talks about where they see themselves on the line scale, share a story of how you came to realize your brokenness. The lawyer arrogantly questioned Jesus. Use Proverbs 11:2 and 16:18 to talk about the destructiveness of pride.

3. Listen to your group members' checked responses. Though each of the responses is valid, spend additional time talking about the following statement: Jesus wanted to show that most people have a narrow opinion of who their neighbor is. We want our neighbors to be the people we love. Jesus expanded this definition to include all people, including our enemies.

4. See commentary in bold after each statement.
   - No one today acts like the Samaritan. **Not everyone does, but there are still good Samaritans out there.**
   - The victim was just asking to be robbed by traveling alone; he didn't deserve help. **We often blame victims as an excuse for not helping them.**
   - There is no reward in being a good Samaritan. **The reward may not be immediate, but you will be storing up treasure in heaven for yourself.**
   - I am more like the Samaritan than the priest or Levite. **Good discussion starter. Ask, "What do you think of the Samaritan's actions?"**

5. This situation identifies your neighbor as someone who is not easy to love.
   Ask, *"What should Donnette say to Sara? Is Sara Donnette's neighbor?"*

6. Talk with your group about some of the people they don't like who are their neighbors and how they can love the unlovable.

CLOSE

Read Luke 10:37 out loud. Jesus helped us expand our definition of *neighbor*. Now we need to "go and do likewise." How we do this will look different for each of us, but we don't want to make excuses or behave selfishly any longer. Let's go love our neighbor.

> *The expert in the law replied, "The one who had mercy on him."*
> *Jesus told him, "Go and do likewise."*
> *(Luke 10:37)*

1. **If your house were on fire, what two things would you rush to save?**

THE STORY OF THE RICH FOOL

The good life isn't about stuff

2. **Do you A (agree) or D (disagree) with each of these statements?**

___ Greed can be good.
___ Wanting more stuff is normal.
___ The more stuff you have, the better you feel about yourself.
___ It's bad to want the things others have.
___ You can never have too much stuff.

3. **If you died today, who would get your stuff?**

- My parents
- It would get thrown away
- I don't even want to think about it
- My brothers/sisters would fight over it
- It would get sold at a yard sale
- It would be kept in a shrine in honor of my memory
- Other: _____

4. **Complete the statement:**

When I can buy _____, I'll have a good life.

5. **On the line scale below, place an X to answer the question.**

How much does our stuff get in the way of our relationship with Christ?

```
          1              2              3              4              5
◆○○○○○○○◆○○○○○○○◆○○○○○○○◆○○○○○○○◆○○○○○○○◆
NOT AT ALL                                        TOTALLY MESSES IT UP
```

6. **Can a person be wealthy and have a healthy, growing relationship with Christ?**

READ OUT LOUD

Two brothers were fighting over their inheritance. It appears that one of the brothers was greedy, cutting the other brother out of a portion of the inheritance or taking a larger share of the inheritance than he needed. Jesus used this occasion to teach his disciples about materialism. Read the story found in Luke 12:13-21.

ASK

If you added up the worth of everything around you right now, how much would it add up to?

DISCUSS, BY THE NUMBERS

1. Get a faith conversation going on the importance (or lack of importance) of the stuff your group members name. After listening to your group's answers, ask, "What do the answers have in common?"

2. See commentary in bold after each statement.
   - Greed can be good. **"Greed is good" is the saying from the famous movie *Wall Street*—then greed took its toll on the economy. Greed is never good. When we're greedy, we think only about ourselves, not the good of our neighbor.**
   - Wanting more stuff is normal. **It is normal in the sense that it is part of our sinful nature.**
   - The more stuff you have, the better you feel about yourself. **Unfortunately true for many of us. But instead of stuff, we need Christ.**
   - It's bad to want the things that others have. **Wanting things isn't necessarily bad; obsessing (what the Tenth Commandment is all about) is bad—especially at the expense of others.**
   - You can never have too much stuff. **In the United States, most people have too much stuff. Ask, "How much stuff is enough?"**

3. This question gets a good faith conversation going about how unimportant much of our stuff really is.

4. The point of this item is to show that the good life is more about relationships and experiences than the stuff we own.

5. Recreate the line scale on a whiteboard or an easel pad. Ask your group members to place their X on the line. Spend time talking realistically and practically about how materialism gets in the way of your relationship with Christ. It keeps the focus on the unimportant while taking the focus off the important—our relationship with our Savior and Lord.

6. Yes, a person can have great wealth and a growing relationship with Jesus, but it's not easy because of how important money can become.

CLOSE

Read Jesus' words from Luke 12:21. Use this closing time to talk about being rich toward God in prayer, Bible reading, faith conversations with friends and family, worship, and other spiritual practices that grow your relationship with Christ.

This is how it will be with those who store up things for themselves but are not rich toward God. —Jesus, in Luke 12:21

THE STORY OF THE RICH MAN & LAZARUS

Closing one's mind to Jesus

1. The rich man "lived in luxury every day" (Luke 16:19). This means that the rich man—

   • was guaranteed happiness because he could buy anything he wanted.
   • might have been happy if he bought the right stuff.
   • was miserable because he would have worried about keeping his wealth.

2. Which one of these statements do you think is most true? The rich man ended up in hell because—

   • his money was the most important thing in his life.
   • you can't be rich and go to heaven.
   • his wealth fooled him into thinking he was in control of his life.
   • great wealth puts your soul at great risk.
   • he was too busy making money to have time for God.
   • he put his trust in his wealth rather than in God.
   • only poor people make it into heaven.
   • he had made up his mind that there was no God, that this world was all there is.

3. Complete this statement:

   Your spiritual choices matter because—

4. If you had the wealth of the rich man in the story, what would you do?

READ OUT LOUD

While today's story didn't actually happen (as is the case with Jesus' parables), it's still important. Jesus has a point to make. (It also means that the Lazarus talked about in the story isn't the Lazarus whom Jesus resurrected.) Read the story from Luke 16:19-31.

ASK

What does it mean to have an open mind? To have a closed mind?

DISCUSS, BY THE NUMBERS

1. The point of this item is to get a faith conversation going about happiness. Remember that happiness is determined by things that happen around us while joy (the kind that Christians experience, anyway) comes from within. One can experience joy no matter what the circumstance.

2. All of the responses could be true. Get your group's opinions regarding each statement. You may want to spend some time on the statement, "great wealth puts your soul at great risk," because money and material things can jeopardize your relationship with Christ.

3. After listening to the completed sentence stems, start a faith conversation about why spiritual choices matter.

4. See what your group members came up with to answer the question. Ask, "What will you do with the wealth you now have?"

CLOSE

Jesus used today's story as a teaching tool to show that our spiritual decisions do matter. Many people close their minds to salvation by faith in Jesus Christ—even though the historical evidence points to the truth of this claim. Yet, they will believe in aliens bringing life to earth or other fanciful ideas. How closed-minded are you? Are you willing to examine the facts of the gospel—that Jesus is who he said he is?

1. When the roof broke open, do you think the people listening to Jesus teach were angry? Do you think Peter, whose house it was, became angry? Do you think Jesus became angry?

2. Respond to each statement with a Y (yes), N (no), or MS (maybe so).

____ The four friends put their trust in Jesus.
____ The average person in the crowd put his trust in Jesus.
____ The healed man put his trust in Jesus.
____ The teachers of the law who were in the crowd put their trust in Jesus.
____ Peter put his trust in Jesus.

3. Answer these two questions:

• Why do you think you need Christian friends of faith like the paralyzed man had?

• Why do you think you need friends who aren't Christians?

4. The paralyzed man was probably very poor. We know this because he lay on a mat typically used by the poor.

What's your opinion?

I think Jesus cared so much for the poor because—

5. Which of these do you think amazed the crowd the most?

❏ Jesus' teachings   ❏ Jesus' miracles   ❏ Jesus' looks

READ OUT LOUD
Jesus was in his disciple Peter's home. This is where Jesus hung out when he was in Capernaum (see Mark 1:29). People quickly learned where Jesus was and jammed into Peter's place to hear Jesus preach. Read what happens next from Mark 2:1-12.

ASK
Which of your friends can burp the loudest? The longest? The weirdest sounding?

DISCUSS, BY THE NUMBERS
Note: Daniel 7:13-14 began the tradition of calling the Messiah "the Son of Man." Jesus calls himself the Son of Man.
1. These three questions will get the conversation going.
2. See commentary in bold after each statement.
   - The four friends put their trust in Jesus. **Probably true. Why else would they have worked so hard to get their friend to Jesus?**
   - The average person in the crowd puts his trust in Jesus. **Maybe so. At least some of them did.**
   - The healed man put his trust in Jesus. **Yes. Jesus confirms this by telling the man that his sins are forgiven.**
   - The teachers of the law in the crowd put their trust in Jesus. **Probably not, based on their response.**
   - **Peter put his trust in Jesus. Yes!**
3. Ask, "Do you have four friends like the paralyzed man had? What are these Christian friends willing to do for you? What are you willing to do for them? Do they help or hinder your relationship with Christ?"
4. Jesus spoke often about helping the poor. The Old Testament also commands us to care for the poor. Jesus was interested in justice, something the poor rarely received. Ask, "How are you looking out for the poor as Jesus did?"

5. Ask, "What surprises you most about Jesus?"

CLOSE
Read Mark 2:12 out loud. What was amazing about this story? Jesus' miracle? Jesus' forgiveness of sin? Jesus proving to the teachers of the law that he was the long-awaited Messiah? All of the above? What is also amazing is that a poor man in ill health had four friends with faith in Jesus who were willing to help him find healing and forgiveness. If you don't remember anything else from today's true story, remember this—we need friends with faith to walk with us, and sometimes even carry us, on our journey of faith.

[The paralyzed man] got up, took his mat and walked out in full view of them all. This amazed everyone and they praised God, saying, "We have never seen anything like this!" (Mark 2:12)

1. What do you think?

- ☐ I haven't brought any pain to my parents.
- ☐ I have brought some pain to my parents.
- ☐ I have brought lots of pain to my parents.

2. The Greek woman, in pain over her daughter's situation, shouts out for Christ to have mercy on her. What do people often do when they are in emotional/spiritual pain?

- ☐ Drink alcohol
- ☐ Stuff the pain inside
- ☐ Smoke marijuana
- ☐ Pray
- ☐ Surf the Net
- ☐ Rage
- ☐ Go shopping
- ☐ Get into fights
- ☐ Cry out to Jesus
- ☐ Exercise
- ☐ Eat/don't eat
- ☐ Sink into depression
- ☐ Read the Bible
- ☐ Do stupid things

3. It's tough to trust Jesus when my life stinks!

☐ Always   ☐ Sometimes   ☐ Never

4. The disciples wanted the woman to stop following Christ. Who or what tries to keep you from following Jesus?

- ☐ My best friend
- ☐ Online friendships
- ☐ My laziness
- ☐ Homework
- ☐ Boyfriend/girlfriend
- ☐ A sin
- ☐ Video games
- ☐ An agnostic teacher
- ☐ Parents
- ☐ Sports

5. What do you think of the following statements? Answer A (always), S (sometimes), or N (never).

___ Jesus is my Santa Claus when I pray.
___ Don't ever give up praying for what you think is God's will.
___ God is to blame when bad things happen to us.
___ Your prayers will be answered if you are good enough.
___ If you show God how desperate you are, your prayers will be answered.

READ OUT LOUD

A Greek woman approaches Jesus with her daughter's sad story of demon possession. Here we have a Gentile, someone outside the Jewish faith, wanting help from the Messiah sent to the Jews. This story is a picture of what is to come—the Jewish nation rejecting Jesus, who then opens up salvation to everyone, Jew *and* Gentile. This daughter was under the influence of Satan. The Bible doesn't say how or why her life was opened to this demonic influence—just that it happened. The mother desperately wanted to help her daughter but was powerless to do so. The pain she experienced over her daughter's situation brought her to Jesus. Read the story found in Mark 7:24-30.

ASK

What is something that you had to try over and over again before you got it right?

DISCUSS, BY THE NUMBERS

1. The Greek woman seemed to be aware of the fact that Jesus came to the Jews first. Yet, her faith kept her persistent. And the pain she felt for her daughter also seemed to motivate her reliance on Jesus as the only hope for her daughter's demonic condition. Use this time to talk about the love most parents have for their children even when their kids are bringing pain into the family through bad choices. Ask, "Why do you think some young people bring pain into their families?" "How does doing this affect their relationship with their parents?"

2. When people experience pain and suffering, they look for relief—often in destructive behaviors such as substance abuse or shopping sprees. The Greek woman in this story turned to Jesus. In fact, she cried out to him again and again. Ask, "When have you cried out to Jesus for mercy?" "How did Christ respond?"

3. Pain and suffering brings people closer or pushes them farther away from Jesus. Ask, "Why do some people push themselves away from God when life gets painful?" "Why is putting your faith in Christ a more appropriate response?"

4. Ask, "Were you surprised the disciples of Christ wanted to get rid of the woman?" Talk about what

keeps your group members from including other believers.

5. See commentary in bold after each statement.

- Jesus is my Santa Claus when I pray. **God is not a heavenly Santa Claus who gives us whatever we want. God provides for our needs in the way that is best for us.**
- Don't ever give up praying for what you think is God's will. **Yes, if we believe our request is honoring to God. Praying for a new toy that we don't need is not honoring God. The woman's request for Christ to cast the demons out of her daughter was God-honoring. When our will and Christ's will are the same, then our prayers are answered with a "yes."**
- God is to blame when bad things happen to us. **The woman never blamed Jesus. She kept requesting that he have mercy on her. We ought to do the same, for it is not the fault of God when we are the victims of evil. Ask, "Why do you think we often blame God for the pain and suffering we see in the world?"**
- Your prayers will be answered if you are good enough. **No one is good enough. All of us fall short of God's standard of holiness. Goodness has nothing to do with our prayer life.**
- If you show God how desperate you are, your prayers will be answered. **One way God teaches us to pray is by requiring us to pray again and again for the same thing. God wants us to be persistent. When we are persistent in prayer, we learn more about God's will for our lives and how to more effectively pray. We may not get what we ask for if what we ask is not God's will.**

CLOSE

Jesus rewarded the faith and persistence of the Greek woman. What she asked for—mercy—was within God's will, and Jesus helped her daughter. God does not hand out goodies to some while striking others with pain and suffering. Our God is love. God waits for us to call on him, asking in faith for mercy. God wants to work in the lives of people who put their trust in him.

1. What's the coolest miracle you could ever see?

2. Do you **A (agree)** or **D (disagree)** with the following statements?

    ___ I'm too young to be able to do anything that could help others.
    ___ I'm too busy to help others.
    ___ I don't want to help others.
    ___ I help others by praying for them.
    ___ Enough grownups help others, so my help is not needed.
    ___ I help others often.
    ___ I can partner with adults to help others.

3. The blind guy's friends brought him to Jesus. How are you bringing your spiritually blind friends to Jesus?

4. What do you think? Place a check in the box of your choice. Christ led the blind guy by the hand away from Bethsaida in order to—

    ❏ get the guy ready to learn more about faith.
    ❏ frighten the guy.
    ❏ find a good place to trip the guy.
    ❏ spark the guy's curiosity.
    ❏ help the guy grow in faith by having to rely on Jesus.
    ❏ rob the guy.

5. Which of the following statements are **T (true)** and which are **F (false)**?

    ___ As the man's sight improved, his faith was strengthened.
    ___ The man's partial vision after the spit was placed in his eyes meant that the guy needed glasses.
    ___ The blind guy was a follower of Jesus.
    ___ The gradual healing process taught the man to trust Jesus.
    ___ The spit in the guy's eyes was gross.

READ OUT LOUD

Christ came to Bethsaida, a town where he performed many miracles, yet the people stubbornly refused to turn to God (Matthew 11:20-21). A few of the people, however, seemed to put their faith in him. They believed that Jesus' touch would heal a blind friend. Interestingly, the blind man does not ask for healing, but his friends beg for Jesus' touch on his behalf. Read the story from Mark 8:22-26.

ASK

What is one life situation that Jesus could best use to help you grow in faith—winning the lottery; being on the cover of a popular magazine; receiving a modeling contract?

DISCUSS, BY THE NUMBERS

1. This question, "What's the coolest miracle you could ever see?" sets the stage for today's faith conversations.

2. Like Christ, we all have opportunities to help others. And as Christians we are compelled by Christ to love our neighbors as ourselves. Identify opportunities your group members have to help others.

3. There are many spiritually blind people around us. Our job is to get them in front of Christ. It is the Holy Spirit's job to do the rest. Encourage your group members to pray for their friends who aren't Christ-followers by listing their names and praying for them daily.

4. Christ prepared the man for his healing by walking him out of town. It prepared the guy to receive the healing by faith and taught him to rely on Christ. Talk about the checked statements.
   - ✔ get the guy ready to learn more about faith
   - ❏ frighten the guy
   - ❏ find a good place to trip the guy
   - ✔ spark the guy's curiosity
   - ✔ help the guy grow in faith by having to rely on Jesus
   - ❏ rob the guy

5. See commentary in bold next to each statement:
   - As the man's sight improved, his faith was strengthened. **This makes sense. The guy's vision was blurred, and then Christ touched his eyes again and he could see clearly. Ask, "Would this process have strengthened your faith in Christ?"**
   - The man's partial vision, after the spit was placed in his eyes, meant that the guy needed glasses. **If Christ had stopped at this point in the healing process, the man would've gone through the rest of his life with blurred vision. Fortunately, for the man, Christ was finished teaching him about faith.**
   - The blind guy was a follower of Jesus. **Christ used the man's blindness and the gradual healing process to grow the man's faith. The blind guy either put his faith in Christ during the healing process or was already a believer in Jesus and the process strengthened his faith.**
   - The gradual healing process taught the man to trust Jesus. **The process may have seemed silly to the man—walking out of town, spit in the eyes and partial vision, and then touched again by Christ to have his vision completely restored. But the man didn't argue with the process or the results!**
   - The spit in the guy's eyes was gross. **Yes, it was. Why Christ used this strategy to heal is anyone's guess. Maybe Jesus wanted to show the man that he needed to rely on Christ for his healing rather than the method of healing.**

CLOSE

Christ used a man's blindness to teach him about faith. In the same way, Christ can use whatever situation in which you find yourself to grow your faith. Ask him today to increase your faith through the situations in your life.

NOTE: Jesus asked the healed man *not* to return to Bethsaida. Since the townspeople had rejected Christ, perhaps Jesus felt that the people would be a bad influence on the man.

1. **What is the greatest thing God has done in your life (other than your salvation)?**

   ❏ God was with me through a difficult time in my life.
   ❏ I was cured of cancer.
   ❏ Nothing.
   ❏ I don't know; I would have to really think about it for a while.
   ❏ God rescued me from a tough situation.

2. **Mark these statements T (true) or F (false)—**

   ___ When you die that's the end. There is nothing more.
   ___ When you die you become an angel if you were good.
   ___ Once you die your spirit lives on as a ghost.
   ___ If you put your faith in Christ, you will be resurrected at the end of time.
   ___ When you die you may come back as another person.

3. **Have you ever known someone who died? Did you go to that person's funeral? Did you go to the cemetery?**

4. **Mark these statements T (true) or F (false)—**

   Lazarus had a near-death experience but didn't really die. _____
   Today's story never really happened. _____
   Jesus bringing Lazarus back to life shows that he can do anything. _____
   Jesus=God. _____
   Lazarus had to die twice. _____

5. **If Jesus could raise Lazarus from the dead, then he can do impossible things in my life.**

   ❏ I'm not good enough for Jesus to do that for me.
   ❏ Maybe if I'm lucky.
   ❏ I wish.
   ❏ He could, but I don't want Jesus working in my life. I haven't finishing sinning yet.
   ❏ Absolutely, and I will pray every day that he does impossible things in my life.

READ OUT LOUD

Lazarus, Jesus' good friend and brother to Martha and Mary, died four days before Jesus went to his hometown. Jesus purposely waited two additional days to come to Lazarus' aid. This way there would be no question that he had, in fact, died. Read what happens in John 11:17-45.

ASK

Who do you know who can do practically anything?

DISCUSS, BY THE NUMBERS

1. Listen to your group members' responses to the question, "What is the greatest thing God has ever done in your life (other than your salvation)?" Discuss the answers.
2. See commentary in bold after each statement.
   - When you die that's the end. There is nothing more. **The Sadducees of Jesus' time didn't believe in the resurrection (that's why they were Sad-you-see). Many believe this today.**
   - When you die you become an angel if you were good. **No, but Hollywood certainly thinks so!**
   - Once you die your spirit lives on as a ghost. **No, but this is a common myth that, again, Hollywood takes advantage of.**
   - If you put your faith in Christ, you will be resurrected at the end of time. **This is what the Bible teaches. There are questions about the "when" but not about the resurrection. The Bible teaches that Christians will be raised to life after we die (1 Corinthians 15:12-21). Even those who haven't put their faith in Christ will be brought back from the dead for judgment (Hebrews 9:27).**
   - When you die you may come back as another person. **This is reincarnation, which the Bible doesn't teach.**
3. Use this item to talk about the reality of death. Everyone will die. And the decisions you make now affect what happens once you die. Also talk about grief. Grief is what happens when we lose something, especially a loved one, to death. It is normal and healthy. But when a believer in Jesus dies, the Bible teaches us that our grief is different because of the hope we have in everlasting life (See 1 Thessalonians 4:13).
4. See commentary in bold after each statement.
   - Lazarus had a near-death experience but didn't really die. **No. He had been dead four days. Near-death experiences today are controversial and not easily provable. They are most likely chemical reactions in the brain due to lack of oxygen. Out-of-body experiences are also likely chemical reactions in the brain.**
   - Today's story never really happened. **If so, then it's possible that the whole Bible is made up.**
   - Jesus bringing Lazarus back to life shows that he can do anything. **A resurrection was considered impossible except by the hand of God. Jesus can do the impossible.**
   - Jesus=God. **Yes, and this miracle, as well as others he performed, proved it.**
   - Lazarus had to die twice. **Yes, he did have to die again.**
5. Prayer requests will come out of the responses made to the statement, "If Jesus could raise Lazarus from the dead, then he can do impossible things in my life." Take time in your group to pray. Encourage your group members to expect to see the resurrection power of Christ at work in their lives.

CLOSE

Today's story is yet another reminder that God can do the impossible—even in our own lives. But as with Martha, Jesus asks us to believe in him for that to happen. We must live like we expect to see the resurrection power of Christ working in our lives.

AN UNBELIEVABLE EXPERIENCE

A taste of heaven can happen here on earth

1. **Place an X on the line below, indicating which direction you're moving in your relationship with Jesus Christ.**

◆○○○○○○○○○○○○○○○○○○○○◆
CLOSER   FARTHER AWAY

2. **Jesus' appearance changed into that of his glorified body—what he now looks like in heaven. You will also get a new body in heaven as Moses and Elijah did.**

	YES	NO
Do you think you will recognize Jesus in heaven?	❑	❑
Do you think you will be happy with your new body in heaven?	❑	❑
Do you think you will recognize your friends in heaven?	❑	❑
Do you think you will recognize your family members in heaven?	❑	❑

3. **What do you think? The disciples got a taste of heaven on the mountaintop.**

   ❑ Yes, and they wanted more of it.
   ❑ Yes, but it scared them.
   ❑ Yes, but they didn't understand it.

4. **Peter was so amazed by what he saw that he wanted to hold on to the moment and construct permanent shelters for Elijah, Moses, and Jesus. What do you think your reaction would have been to this sight?**

   ❑ I would be ready to help Peter.
   ❑ I would be hiding.
   ❑ I would be standing there with my mouth open.
   ❑ I would have a list of questions ready to ask Moses and Elijah.
   ❑ Other:_____

5. **The cloud represented the presence of God on the mountaintop. God's voice, coming from the cloud, repeated what he said at Jesus' baptism with an additional command: "Listen to him!"**

   These three disciples needed to hear God say this so that—

READ OUT LOUD

Jesus goes up to a mountaintop with the three disciples closest to him—Peter, James, and John. There, he is transformed into his heavenly state and talks with Moses and Elijah about his coming death and resurrection. The whole experience is a little taste of heaven here on earth for the three disciples. Read the story in Matthew 17:1-8.

ASK

What dessert have you eaten that tasted like a slice of heaven?

DISCUSS, BY THE NUMBERS

1. Jesus chooses to share the moment of his transfiguration with his three closest disciples. Use the line scale to talk about the kind of relationship your group members have and want to have with Jesus.

2. Get a faith conversation going about what it will be like to see Jesus in heaven. Yes, we will be able to recognize family and friends in heaven. Your group members may talk about what their glorified bodies will be like—bodies that will last through eternity. They may want to talk about their family and friends who will also be in heaven. There are some of your group members who will talk about family and friends who haven't put their faith in Christ and will wonder what becomes of them. Use this as an opportunity to talk about sharing Christ with family and friends who aren't Christians. For a good explanation of our heavenly bodies, read 1 Corinthians 15:35-58.

3. All three statements are true.

4. Ask, "Would you have wanted to keep this little taste of heaven going if you were Peter?" Create a list of the questions your group members would want to ask Moses and Elijah. See what kinds of answers your group members come up with.

5. Hearing the voice of God certainly affected the three disciples. Talk about what it would do to the faith of your group members. Ask, "Why do you think God, the Father, repeats what he said to Jesus at the beginning of his ministry, here on the mountaintop, as Jesus' ministry on earth is drawing to a close?" One possible answer: To strengthen the faith of the three disciples so they could lead the other disciples in spreading the good news after Christ's death and resurrection.

CLOSE

The bodies we have now are wasting away due to sin that began with Adam and Eve. But at the end of time, everyone who died in Christ will be resurrected and receive new bodies that will last forever. Until then we receive glimpses of heaven here on earth as we do our Lord's work.

1. How self-centered was the younger son? Check one.

- ❏ Very self-centered
- ❏ Somewhat self-centered
- ❏ Not at all self-centered

2. I've known people like the younger son who have made disastrous decisions.

- ❏ I've seen them on TV and in movies.
- ❏ I've read stories about them.
- ❏ I've known them personally.
- ❏ I've been one of them.

3. There are consequences to pay for wild living.

Agree   Disagree

4. Why must we sometimes "work with pigs" before we learn a life lesson?

- ❏ It takes pain for us to learn.
- ❏ We must experience this for ourselves.
- ❏ We think this only happens to other people.
- ❏ We think we are smarter than those people.
- ❏ We don't care about consequences.

5. For which of the following situations do you think you need to say you're sorry?

- ❏ Getting angry at a bully
- ❏ Lying to a parent
- ❏ Stealing from a convenience store
- ❏ Ditching a class at school
- ❏ Skipping a church service to sleep in
- ❏ Hitting your sister or brother

6. What's your opinion?

- ❏ God loves me as much as the father loved the son in this story.
- ❏ God loves me almost as much as the father in this story.
- ❏ God loves me when I'm good.
- ❏ God can only take so much, and then he will stop loving me.
- ❏ I'm not sure God loves me.

AN UNBELIEVABLE STORY

God's love for us is immeasurable

READ OUT LOUD

In today's story, a younger son demands his inheritance from his father. With his wealth in hand, he heads off as far as he can from his family to a foreign country where he can party guilt-free apart from their presence. You can read the story from Luke 15:11-32.

ASK

How do you know when a parent loves you?

DISCUSS, BY THE NUMBERS

1. The younger son was unwilling to wait until his father's death to receive his inheritance—a selfish act. The younger son represents sinners who want to separate themselves from God's loving presence and live like they, instead of God, are in control of their lives. Use this item to discuss how you and your group members are like the younger son.

2. Talk about some of the disastrous decisions and their consequences. Ask, "Why do you think God allows us to make bad, even disastrous, decisions like the youngest son made?" The answer: Our Father in heaven gave us free will to make moral choices that lead to life or death—it's our decision. So, too, the father in the story never protested his younger son's departure. He freely gave him his share of the wealth and let him go on his way.

3. Talk about the consequences that we pay for our sins; the unwillingness of Hollywood and pop culture to accurately portray consequences (notice that in the movies the natural consequences of sin are often downplayed); and the grace available to us from God.

4. See commentary in bold after each statement. "Working with the pigs" is a consequence of sin that we often have to pay in order to learn a lesson.

   Interesting note: In the Old Testament, God forbade Israel to eat pig meat. This was for their own protection. In warm climates, like that of the Middle East, pork often carried diseases and parasites. When humans consumed the diseased meat, it often led to severe sickness and physical disorders (see Leviticus 11:7). This fact makes "working with pigs" all the more important. Jesus' Jewish audience would've certainly picked up on the pig reference and taken it as evidence regarding just how far this young man had fallen from the good life he knew with his father.

☐ It takes pain for us to learn. **Often this is true, but we can also learn from watching the pain caused by the sins of others.**

☐ We must experience this for ourselves. **We don't have to "work with pigs" to learn a life lesson. We can learn from the stories of the Bible.**

☐ We think this only happens to other people. **Yes, we often think that "working with pigs" happens to other people. We won't get caught.**

☐ We think we are smarter than those people. **Again, yes. Somehow we think we're smart enough to avoid the consequences of sin.**

☐ We don't care about consequences. **Sometimes we don't until they happen.**

5. Debate which actions (and perhaps all) warrant repentance.

6. We are loved by God as much as the father loved the prodigal son.

CLOSE

The story of the *Prodigal Son* could have been called *A Father's Incredible Love*. The focus of today's story is on God's readiness to freely accept those who are lost, those who are sinners, those who are ready to admit their brokenness. Each of us is the younger son—far away from home until we come to our senses, humbly come before our Father in heaven, and beg forgiveness. God is ready to accept everyone, no matter what their past, into his loving arms.

The younger son represented the sinners in Jesus' day—the ones rejected by the Pharisees and religious leaders. The older son represented the Pharisees—outwardly righteous, but inwardly unrepentant and rejecting the love of the father.

While we are all like the younger son, we often act like the older son, too—unwilling to accept and forgive those who need God's grace the most. We believe we are somehow better than others, not needing at all to ask for God's grace.

So we are both the younger and the older sons depending upon the day of the week, or maybe even the hour of the day. And for both sons, God's love is immeasurable!

THE MEAL

Remembering the purpose of Communion

1. Our church serves Communion...

    a) Only on special occasions
    b) Sporadically
    c) Once a month
    d) Every Sunday
    e) I have no idea

2. Why do you think churches serve Communion? (You can check more than one.)

❏ So that people can get into heaven
❏ To let the world know what Jesus did for us
❏ So that the pastor can keep his/her job
❏ In order for church members to get forgiveness of their sins
❏ Because people are hungry
❏ So that the church members are reminded they are part of God's family
❏ Because Jesus asked the church to do this
❏ To remember the first Good Friday
❏ As an appetizer for lunch
❏ To remind Christians that Jesus died and rose again

3. What do you think you should do while Communion is being served?

❏ Think about lunch
❏ Pray for forgiveness
❏ Listen to my mp3 player
❏ Pray that God will shape me to be more like Jesus
❏ Plot revenge on someone who hurt me
❏ Feel guilty
❏ Text friends
❏ Worry
❏ Catch up on sleep
❏ Be grateful for God's grace

4. What do you like most about the Communion service at your church? What do you like least? What would you most want to see changed?

5. Jesus said the cup of wine was like this covenant, or agreement, God made with us. The agreement says God will forgive our sins, but we must choose to accept this forgiveness by faith. Check the statement below you agree with most:

❏ I have put my faith in Jesus so that my sins are forgiven.
❏ I am thinking about putting my faith in Jesus.
❏ I will never put my faith in Jesus.
❏ There is no Jesus.

READ OUT LOUD

The first Communion ever celebrated was the last meal Jesus had with his disciples before his death. The first Communion reminds us of the first Easter. The first Communion reminds us of all that Jesus has done for us. Read the story of the first Communion from Matthew 26:17-19, 26-30.

ASK

What's your favorite meal?

DISCUSS, BY THE NUMBERS

1. Begin your Communion discussion by talking about the number of occasions your congregation celebrates Communion. Talk about why your church serves Communion as much or as little as it does.
2. See commentary in bold after each statement.
   - So that people can get into heaven. **Communion has nothing to do with a ticket to heaven.**
   - To let the world know what Jesus did for us. **Communion around the world proclaims the good news.**
   - So that the pastor can keep his/her job. **No, the pastor has plenty to do besides serving Communion.**
   - In order for church members to get forgiveness of their sins. **Communion celebrates the forgiveness of our sins, but the act does not obtain forgiveness for us.**
   - Because people are hungry. **No, Communion doesn't provide enough bread or drink to satisfy hunger. The Corinthian church members were supposed to eat before they came to church so they wouldn't be hungry and devour the Communion elements as a meal (1 Corinthians 11:20-28).**
   - So that the church members are reminded that they are part of God's family. **Yes, Communion celebrates our membership in the body of Christ.**
   - Because Jesus asked the church to do this. **Yes, Christ asked us to regularly take Communion to remember him and what he did.**
   - To remember the first Good Friday. **The first Communion happened on the Thursday night before Good Friday.**
   - As an appetizer for lunch. **It's easy to sometimes take Communion and think about lunch if it is served before noon.**
   - To remind Christians that Jesus died and rose again. **It certainly is a great reminder of Jesus' sacrifice.**
3. Lead a discussion on how we ought to act while taking Communion. Should we pray? Reflect on our lives? Ask for forgiveness? Be grateful for God's grace?
4. Talk about the most and least liked parts of Communion, as well as what changes your group members would like to see. Decide if this is something worth discussing with your congregation's pastor.
5. This item gives you a chance to share the gospel with anyone in the group who may be new or is unclear of the good news about Jesus.

CLOSE

Our church is like a family who cares for and needs each other. One of the traditions of our church family is Communion. This tradition, started by Jesus himself, is something we are to do in remembrance of him until his return (see 1 Corinthians 11:26).

1. **John begins today's story telling us that Jesus loved the disciples. How did John know this?**

   ❏ He was guessing.
   ❏ He experienced it.
   ❏ He looked it up in the Bible.
   ❏ He knew it was the right answer.
   ❏ His parents told him.

2. **What do you think it would be like for you to wash others' dirty feet?**

   ❏ Gross
   ❏ Humbling
   ❏ Demeaning—I would feel like their servant
   ❏ Energizing
   ❏ Frustrating
   ❏ Embarrassing
   ❏ Depressing

3. **Which of the 12 disciples are you most like?**

   ❏ I'm like Judas, who, a short time later, sold Jesus out.
   ❏ I'm like the ten disciples (not Judas or Peter) who said nothing, just sat there as Jesus lowered himself to the status of a household servant.
   ❏ I'm like Peter, who spoke up because he was ashamed that Jesus lowered himself to servant status and washed the disciples' feet instead of one of them doing it.

4. **Who is the humblest person in your church? How is this person like Jesus? What have you learned from watching this person?**

5. **TOUGH QUESTION: What was Jesus trying to teach you by washing the disciples' feet?**

6. **The foot-washing exercise was a great picture of what Jesus did for you on the cross. How often do you need to be reminded that you are filthy?**

   ❏ All the time. I easily forget my brokenness or sinfulness.
   ❏ Sometimes. It is easy to forget that I need Jesus.
   ❏ Never. I'm always aware that I need Christ.
   ❏ But I'm a good person.

READ OUT LOUD
Filled with pride, none of the 12 disciples volunteered to wash the feet of Jesus or any other feet, for that matter. It was the custom of the day that the servant of the house would wash the dusty feet of guests. So guess who played house servant to the embarrassment of the disciples? Read the story found in John 13:1-17.

ASK
Would you rather have someone serve you by cleaning your room or doing your homework?

DISCUSS, BY THE NUMBERS
1. See commentary in bold after each statement.
   - He was guessing. **He was not guessing because John was there with Jesus. Remember, this is John, the disciple of Jesus, not John the Baptist who prepared the way for Jesus.**
   - He experienced it. **Yes, as one of the three disciples closest to Jesus (the other two were Peter and James), John experienced Jesus' love firsthand.**
   - He looked it up in the Bible. **The complete Bible had not yet been written.**
   - He knew it was the right answer. *Jesus* or *Jesus loves you* **is often the answer to many of our deepest theological questions, but this is not why John knew of Jesus' love.**
   - His parents told him. **No, he had to experience it.**
2. Through a show of hands, find out which of the words was chosen the most. Then discuss how Christ must have felt while washing his disciples' feet. Ask, "How did washing the disciples' feet show that Jesus loved them?"
3. Take this time to compare yourself to the 12 disciples. Then use this as a springboard to discuss where your group members see themselves.
4. Use these two questions to get your group members discussing what humility looks like.

5. This tough question hopefully challenges you and your group members to seriously look at the lesson learned. Ask, "So what?" "How will today's story make a difference in your life tomorrow?"
6. The foot-washing exercise was a great picture of what Jesus did for you on the cross. How often do you need to be reminded that you are filthy?

CLOSE
Jesus is the true servant-leader. Jesus is the ultimate picture of true humility. Jesus did what the disciples refused. And now we have a choice. Will we act like Jesus and demonstrate humility in our thoughts and actions?

PETER'S DENIAL PREDICTED

Through actions and words we affirm our devotion to Jesus

1. Jesus predicts that all 11 disciples (Judas, the 12th disciple, sells him out) will abandon him on the night of his arrest. When are you most likely to abandon Jesus?

- ❏ When things are going great in my life
- ❏ When my life is falling apart
- ❏ When I have everything I need
- ❏ When someone I know has died
- ❏ When I commit a big sin
- ❏ When a friend of mine is hurting
- ❏ When I desperately need something
- ❏ When I get good grades
- ❏ When my parents aren't arguing
- ❏ When someone is spreading a rumor about me

2. How likely do you think it is that you will ever abandon Christ?

___ It will happen
___ It might happen
___ It probably won't happen
___ It will never happen

3. "You go to church?" Adam asked.

"Yes," Robert responded, not really sure which way this conversation was going to go.

"So your parents make you go, right? They make you do all this Jesus stuff?" asked Adam.

"No, not really, I kind of like going. You have a problem with that?" asked Robert, suddenly feeling like he needed to defend his church attendance.

"No, Robert," said Adam. "No problem."

Peter felt like he would never abandon Jesus, no matter what the other disciples did. Do you think Robert felt like Peter? Have you ever felt like this?

4. What do you think?

- ❏ I always act like I don't know Jesus.
- ❏ Like Peter, I've acted like I didn't know Jesus at least three times.
- ❏ I once acted like I didn't know Jesus, regretted it, and have never done it again.
- ❏ I've never acted like I didn't know Jesus.

5. Complete these sentence stems—

-I demonstrate my devotion to Christ by what I say when...

-I demonstrate my devotion to Christ by what I do when...

READ OUT LOUD

In this story, Jesus' prediction of Peter's denial is what's usually remembered. But the larger story is a picture of all the disciples' abandonment of Christ. It is also the story of our choice—what will we do with Jesus? Read the story from Matthew 26:31-35. This story is also told in Mark 14:27-31, Luke 22:31-34, and John 13:36-38.

ASK

What do you predict high school will be like?

DISCUSS, BY THE NUMBERS

1. A pattern usually emerges in which people are more likely to abandon Jesus when things are going well but get closer to Christ when things are going south. Talk about ways in which your group members can keep their faith in Christ energized in both good and bad times.

2. Jesus encouraged the disciples by saying to them he would see them again after his death. ("After I have risen, I will go ahead of you into Galilee." —Matthew 26:32) He was saying, "Listen up, don't lose confidence in me. I will rise from the dead! I will allow myself to be crucified, but evil won't prevail." Take time to talk about the fact that Jesus is always there for us but that is not an excuse for us to abandon him (even though there may be times in our lives when we will).

3. This item gets at Peter's confidence that, no matter what happened, he would not walk away from Christ, even if others did. Ask, "What can we learn from Peter's experience?"

4. Eventually, all the disciples except John and Judas died a martyr's death. (Judas committed suicide soon after selling Jesus out.) But John was left to take care of Mary, Jesus' mother. The disciples had told Jesus on the night of his arrest that they were ready to die for him. Yet, that commitment evaporated almost instantly. Ask, "How can we maintain and grow our relationship with Christ in times of adversity and prosperity?"

5. Jesus, not confident at all in Peter's devotion to him, predicted that Peter would deny knowing him three times before morning. It happened just as Jesus said it would. Talk about how your group members can demonstrate their devotion to Jesus in both word and deed.

CLOSE

Through our actions and words we affirm our devotion to Christ. The disciples were willing to do the same until the moment of truth arrived. Relying on their own strength, they walked (and ran) away from Jesus; but after the resurrection and the coming of the Holy Spirit, their devotion to Christ in word and deed remained strong. We can do the same by relying on the Holy Spirit, the encouragement we get from each other, and the spiritual practices of prayer, Bible reading, worship, and service.

1. Which causes you the most pain—a bad haircut or a bad case of the flu?

2. Which of the following actions by the soldiers do you think caused Jesus the most pain before he was crucified?

❑ Beating him with a whip
❑ Stripping him of his outer clothes
❑ Placing a red robe on him
❑ Pushing a crown of thorns on his head
❑ Hitting him repeatedly with a stick that was supposed to be his kingly scepter
❑ Bowing on their knees before Jesus, mocking him as the King of the Jews
❑ Spitting on him

3. What do you think? Read the statements and respond with **A (agree)** or **D (disagree)**.

____ Most of my friends don't know that Jesus suffered and died for them.
____ The pain that Jesus experienced at the hands of the soldiers was not that extreme.
____ People in other countries suffer more than people in the United States and Canada do for their faith in Jesus.
____ The soldiers who made fun of Jesus will go to hell.
____ The suffering Christ endured nearly 2,000 years ago doesn't matter that much today.

4. What can we learn from Jesus' willingness to suffer so much before and during his time on the cross?

❑ Jesus wants us to feel sorry for him.
❑ Jesus' love for us is immeasurable.
❑ Jesus had a high tolerance for pain, so it was no big deal.
❑ Jesus didn't know he would have to suffer so much, or he wouldn't have let himself be arrested.
❑ Jesus naively thought Pilate wouldn't allow the soldiers to hurt him.

5. I have been made fun of for being a follower of Christ—

❑ Many times
❑ A few times
❑ Never

From *More Middle School TalkSheets on the New Testament: 52 Ready-to-Use Discussions* by David Lynn. Permission to reproduce this page granted only for use in buyer's youth group. Copyright © 2010 by Youth Specialties. www.youthspecialties.com

READ OUT LOUD

After Pilate freed Barabbas, a known criminal, he had Jesus severely beaten and given to soldiers for execution by brutal crucifixion. While preparations were being made for Jesus' crucifixion, the soldiers, well…you can read the story found in Matthew 27:26-31.

ASK

Which group gets made fun of the most at your school?

DISCUSS, BY THE NUMBERS

1. This item gets your group talking about pain that they have experienced, which will lead into the discussion of the pain Christ experienced before he even went to the cross.
2. Use this item to talk about why Jesus had to suffer before going to the cross—to fulfill prophecy (Psalm 129:3; Isaiah 50:6; Isaiah 53:5).
3. See commentary in bold after each statement.
   • Most of my friends don't know that Jesus suffered and died for them. **Ask, "Why don't they know about Jesus?" Encourage, without condemning, your group members to talk with their friends about their faith.**
   • The pain that Jesus experienced at the hands of the soldiers was not that extreme. **The pain suffered at the hands of the Roman soldiers was barbaric.**
   • People in other countries suffer more than people in the United States and Canada do for their faith in Jesus. **Citizens of the United States and Canada can be grateful for the freedom of religion available to them.**
   • The soldiers who made fun of Jesus will go to hell. **Scripture is clear. God doesn't want anyone condemned but desires that everyone place their faith in Jesus, including the Roman soldiers.**

• The suffering Christ endured nearly 2,000 years ago doesn't matter that much today. **It matters as much today as when it happened.**
4. Jesus' immeasurable love is demonstrated by his willingness to suffer so much before and during his time on the cross.
5. Talk about the fact that committed Christians will be made fun of at times for their faith in Jesus. The Bible promises this!

CLOSE

[Leader: Tell a story about a time you were made fun of for being a Christ-follower]. Today's story showed how Jesus was made fun of and suffered. And those of us who choose to live for Jesus will find ourselves in situations where we will be made fun of and suffer for our faith as well. Count it a blessing to suffer for Christ, given what he did for you.

ON THE CROSS

Jesus died for our wrongdoing

1. Criminals who were executed by crucifixion had their crimes written on a sign posted above their heads. What crime did the Roman government accuse Jesus of committing?

   ❏ Robbery and murder like the criminals on either side of him
   ❏ Not paying taxes
   ❏ Being the King of the Jews
   ❏ Being a really cool guy
   ❏ Being God

2. Do you think this statement is true or false? Why?

   Jesus had already demonstrated that he was God and didn't need to again prove his divinity with a miracle to those who asked for one.

3. People made fun of Jesus because he claimed to be God but then couldn't save himself from dying on a wooden cross. What do you think?

   ❏ Yes, Jesus is God.
   ❏ Jesus was a liar who claimed to be God but wasn't.
   ❏ Jesus thought he was God because he was psycho.
   ❏ Jesus was plotting to deceive people with his disciples by faking his death on the cross.

4. What do you think? Answer Yeah (I agree), Nah (I disagree), or Duh (I don't know).

   _____ Only big sins needed to be paid for by death.
   _____ Christ died for my sins and for his sins also.
   _____ There are people who refuse to accept the forgiveness of sin Christ offers them.
   _____ If Jesus decided not to die, God could still have forgiven us of our sins.
   _____ Only the sins that you committed before you put your faith in Christ are forgiven. Once you believe in Jesus, you can't sin anymore.

5. Look up Psalm 22:1. Jesus quoted this verse when he was on the cross. Why?

   ❏ Jesus enjoyed quoting Bible verses.
   ❏ Jesus was in so much pain he didn't know what he was saying.
   ❏ Jesus carried so many of the world's sins that it felt like God had turned his back on him.
   ❏ Jesus was getting ready for a Bible verse quiz show.

6. The curtain that separated the most holy place—where God would appear only to the priest—from the rest of the temple was torn into two pieces. What do you think of the following statement?

   With the ripping in two of the temple curtain, I can now approach God through Jesus directly.

   ❏ No, I still need my pastor to go before God for me.
   ❏ Yes, but I shouldn't go into God's presence that often.
   ❏ Yes, but God is really angry with me, so I won't.
   ❏ Yes, I can go directly into God's presence.

READ OUT LOUD

Crucifixion was a gruesome punishment used by the Roman Empire to execute criminals. The cross was made of wood in the form of either a T or an X. The criminal was either nailed or tied to the wooden beams and suffered sometimes for days before dying. Read the crucifixion story of Jesus from Matthew 27:35-54. The story is also told from different perspectives in the other three gospels.

ASK

What will it say on your tombstone?

DISCUSS, BY THE NUMBERS

1. The crime he was accused of was being the King of the Jews—a lie told by the religious leaders so the Roman authorities would have to do something about Jesus. If Jesus aspired to be the Jewish king, then he would be guilty of attempting to overthrow the Roman Empire. Jesus never, ever said he was the King of the Jews or that his mission was a political and military one designed to overthrow Rome.

2. The people making fun of Jesus while he hung on the cross called for a miracle. But Jesus had spent his ministry demonstrating his divinity. The cross was not the time for miracles but the time for atonement for sin. The Jews knew sin required atonement but didn't recognize Christ as the Messiah who was this atonement.

3. Yes, Jesus is God. He is the way, the truth, and the life. If he wasn't God, then he was a liar, or a psycho, or a deceiver. He wasn't simply a good man or a moral role model since liars and psychos aren't the best of either.

4. See commentary in bold after each statement:
   • Only big sins need to be paid for by death. **Nah. All sins, big and little, miss God's mark of holiness, and payment is required.**
   • Christ died for my sins and for his sins also. **Nah. Christ was sinless so he could die for your sins.**
   • There are people who refuse to accept the forgiveness of sin Christ offers them. **Yeah. Why would they do this? There are a number of reasons. A few of those reasons are listed here: They don't think their sins are bad enough. They think the good they do outweighs the bad. They believe people are basically good and don't need to deal with their sin.**
   • If Jesus decided not to die, God could still have forgiven us of our sins. **Nah. God's holy nature required the death of a perfect human. So only the death of Jesus, who chose to take on human flesh, but remained sinless, could satisfy God's holy requirement.**
   • Only the sins that you committed before you put your faith in Christ are forgiven. Once you believe in Jesus, you can't sin anymore. **Nah, Jesus died for all of your sins 2,000 years ago.**

5. The answer: Jesus carried so many of the world's sins that it felt like God had turned his back on him. God's hatred of sin is so great that, in a way not explained in the Bible, God turned away from Jesus because of this burden of sin (not his own sin but ours) he carried.

6. The fact is we have the privilege of direct access to the presence of God because of what Christ did on the cross.

CLOSE

All of your sins, and trillions of other sins, contributed to the suffering Christ felt that made him cry out to God in verse 46, "My God, my God, why have you forsaken me?" Since Christ gave his life for you and me, how should we live for him?

JESUS BURIED

Don't be deceived by the world

1. Respond to each of these questions.

How would you feel if you were Joseph and risked your popularity to bury Jesus?
- ❏ I wouldn't care what others thought of me.
- ❏ I would be really worried about losing my friends.

How would you feel if you were Joseph and risked losing your money to bury Jesus?
- ❏ I wouldn't care if I lost everything.
- ❏ I would be really worried about losing all my stuff.

2. Pilate gave the body of Jesus to Joseph because...

- ❏ he wanted to pocket the money saved on Jesus' burial.
- ❏ he was a secret Christian.
- ❏ he felt guilty for having killed an innocent man to keep the religious leaders happy.
- ❏ he wanted to take off on his vacation.

3. When Joseph laid Jesus in his unused tomb, an Old Testament prophecy predicting the Messiah would be buried with the rich was fulfilled (Isaiah 53:9). It matters that Jesus fulfilled all the Old Testament prophecies because...

a) it shows how clever the disciples were at making sure all the prophecies came true so that they could fake people out about Jesus.
b) it means that there will be another Messiah coming soon to Israel.
c) it means that other religions can save us.
d) it tells us that Jesus is definitely the promised Savior.

4. How would you respond to this statement—true or false?

If Jesus was buried in the tomb by Joseph on Friday afternoon and rose early Sunday morning, then he was not in the grave for three days.

5. The tomb was sealed, guarded, and protected by a large rock so that none of the disciples could steal the body and fake a resurrection.

- The disciples did fake a resurrection, which means Christianity is untrue.
  - ❏ I agree ❏ I disagree ❏ I'm clueless

- People want to believe that there was no resurrection because if it were true, then Jesus is who is said he is.
  - ❏ I agree ❏ I disagree ❏ I'm clueless

- Jesus faked his death, and his body was never put into the tomb.
  - ❏ I agree ❏ I disagree ❏ I'm clueless

- The resurrection was made up on a bet to see if people would fall for it.
  - ❏ I agree ❏ I disagree ❏ I'm clueless

- The resurrection really happened. Jesus is alive.
  - ❏ I agree ❏ I disagree ❏ I'm clueless

- Jesus is the Savior of the world even if the world doesn't want to believe it.
  - ❏ I agree ❏ I disagree ❏ I'm clueless

READ OUT LOUD

The world loves to be deceptive when it comes to the truth. And since Jesus is the truth, there will be deception by those who don't want to hear or believe that truth. So they make up their own truth—like calling Jesus a liar or…well, you need to read the story for yourself, which is found in Matthew 27:57-66.

ASK

How many funerals have you attended?

DISCUSS, BY THE NUMBERS

1. Jesus was dead. The Sabbath, a day of rest, would be starting at sundown. Joseph, and his helper Nicodemus of John 3 (see John 19:39), needed to get Jesus in the tomb before nightfall so that his body would not be burned or buried in the criminals' cemetery. Joseph stepped up and bravely took responsibility for Jesus' remains. Use this as a backdrop to talk about what you and your group members are willing to risk for Jesus. For more information on Joseph see Luke 23:50-51.

2. Pilate gave the body of Jesus to Joseph because…he felt guilty for having killed an innocent man to keep the religious leaders happy. Talk about ways you and your group members have been guilty of treating Jesus badly. Ask, "What did you do with your guilt over treating Jesus badly?"

3. See commentary in bold after each statement.
   - It shows how clever the disciples were at making sure they all came true so that they could fake people out about Jesus. **No, this could not have happened. Most prophecies were outside their control.**
   - It means that there will be another Messiah coming soon to Israel. **No, but some of the orthodox Jews believe the Messiah hasn't come yet, but will.**
   - It means that other religions can save us. **Not at all.**
   - It tells us that Jesus is definitely the promised Savior. **Yes, and you are encouraged to look at Isaiah 53 with your group members.**

4. The statement is false, and here's why. The Jewish people counted part of a day as one day. The new day started at sundown, which means Friday afternoon when Jesus died and was placed in the tomb was Day One. Saturday was Day Two. And Sunday morning, when Jesus rose from the dead, was Day Three. Don't let the world deceive you into thinking that the Bible is wrong. Check out the facts.

5. See commentary in bold after each statement.
   - The disciples did fake a resurrection, which means Christianity is untrue. **Disagree. There is no way this could have happened with the tomb sealed, guarded, and protected with a huge rock (not to mention scared disciples, most of whom abandoned Jesus in his hour of need).**
   - People want to believe that there was no resurrection because if it were true, then Jesus is who is said he is. **Agree. There are some people who don't want to give up control of their lives to God and want to find a reason that the resurrection is untrue.**
   - Jesus faked his death, and his body was never put into the tomb. **Disagree. He was too weak and lost too much blood through the torture they put him through to fake his death.**
   - The resurrection was made up on a bet to see if people would fall for it. **Disagree. There is no evidence to support this.**
   - The resurrection really happened. **Jesus is alive. Agree. That's where all the evidence leads.**
   - Jesus is the Savior of the world even if the world doesn't want to believe it. **Agree. So let's keep sharing the good news of Jesus' love and forgiveness.**

CLOSE

Many in the world want Jesus' resurrection to be untrue. Some believe he never existed or, if he did, he was just a good, moral person or a prophet sent from God—but not God in the flesh. So you will hear things like, "The resurrection was faked!" But how could it have been faked? Jesus had to have died on the cross. The soldier stabbed him in the side to make sure Jesus' heart had stopped beating. That's why water and blood poured out of his side—his heart was not working to circulate the blood. And because the soldier saw that Jesus was already dead, he did not need to break Jesus' legs to speed up the dying process. The tomb was sealed and guarded by Roman soldiers. There is no way the scared disciples would have dared approach the tomb—not to mention fight and overpower deadly soldiers. Jesus died. Jesus was in a guarded tomb. Jesus is no longer in the tomb. So yes, Jesus rose again. Jesus is alive.

ON THE ROAD

Jesus is everywhere if we only open our eyes

1. **The two men were talking about Jesus together. I talk about Jesus with other Christians...**

   - ❏ every chance I get
   - ❏ only if they bring it up first
   - ❏ never
   - ❏ with others at church
   - ❏ with my family
   - ❏ quietly so no one else will hear
   - ❏ through text messages
   - ❏ only in my head
   - ❏ only if forced

2. **The two men on the road were disillusioned and down by the death of Jesus. They had their expectations crushed about who he was and what he would do for them. Have you ever been disappointed by what you thought Jesus would do for you?**

   - ❏ Oh yeah, all the time
   - ❏ Once
   - ❏ Sometimes
   - ❏ Never

3. **If Christ walked along the road with me and a friend, I would ask him...**

   - ❏ to explain how to be saved.
   - ❏ to tell me what career I should pursue.
   - ❏ where to get the best Mexican food.
   - ❏ how I could be more motivated to read the Bible.
   - ❏ to tell us what heaven will be like.
   - ❏ how to fix my family life.
   - ❏ what I should do to be more faithful to him.

4. **Jesus didn't make the two men on the road spend time with him. They had to invite him to stay. What have you invited Jesus to do in your life?**

   I have asked Jesus to...

   - ❏ be my Savior.
   - ❏ help me let go of a sin that won't leave me alone.
   - ❏ help my family.
   - ❏ leave me alone.
   - ❏ help me live for him each day.
   - ❏ heal someone I know.
   - ❏ take charge of my life.
   - ❏ other: _____

5. **Decide if the presence of Christ is A (abundantly clear) or D (difficult to see) in each of the following.**

   - ___ In family life
   - ___ Throughout our schools
   - ___ In our cities
   - ___ In the movies
   - ___ In music
   - ___ In government
   - ___ In our churches
   - ___ On television
   - ___ On the news
   - ___ At sporting events

6. **Christ departed, leaving the two men grateful and pleased that he had spent time with them explaining the Scriptures. How do you feel after spending time studying Scripture with others?**

READ OUT LOUD

The Sunday of Jesus' resurrection, two men were walking along the road to Emmaus, a town outside of Jerusalem. One was a follower of Christ named Cleopas, and the other, many scholars believe, was Luke. Neither of them were part of the original 12 disciples. But just as you are a disciple of Christ because you are a follower of Christ, they too were both disciples. See what happens by reading the story from Luke's account in chapter 24:13-35.

ASK

What is the farthest you've ever been away from home?

DISCUSS, BY THE NUMBERS

1. Use this item to discuss how and why community is the best environment in which to grow in our faith. Christianity is not something we do by ourselves. We really do need each other for worship, encouragement, growth in God's Word, fellowship, and the like.

2. Jesus is a disappointment only when we try to play God and put him in a box. It's like we create a make-believe Jesus who fits all our ideas of who Jesus should be and what he should do for us. But Jesus isn't a disappointment when we accept him as he has been revealed to us in Scripture. The two men on the road felt Jesus didn't save Israel from the Romans (Luke 24:21). That's what they wanted him to do. But Jesus had a different plan. He wanted to give them a new life, a new relationship with God, a new way to live that included forgiveness of their sins.

> *But we had hoped that he was the one who was going to redeem Israel. And what is more, it is the third day since all of this took place.*
> *(Luke 24:21, NIV)*

3. Use this item to talk about the "walk" your group members have with Jesus. Do they understand what it means to "walk" with Jesus (to have a relationship with him where he guides their lives, encourages them, helps them deal with their sins)?

4. Jesus never forces himself on anyone. If you want Jesus, you must ask for him. Talk about what it means to invite Jesus into your life—to have a relationship with him.

5. Use each of these statements to talk about how your group members see Jesus working in each of the settings. Ask, "How do you see yourself fitting in where Jesus is working?"

6. Use this time to talk about the need for personal Bible study as well as Bible study with others. Ask, "What do you get out of studying the Bible by yourself?" "With others?"

CLOSE

Jesus is everywhere if we only open our eyes. Jesus was present with the two men on the road to Emmaus even when they didn't recognize him. Jesus is present at the soup kitchen. Jesus is present in the White House. Jesus is working in our lives and in the lives of others. Jesus invites us to join him in all that he is doing around the world.

JESUS APPEARS TO 10 DISCIPLES

Christ is our living hope

1. Mary Magdalene left the empty tomb and went to tell the disciples that she had seen the resurrected Lord. If you were Mary and this story happened today, who would be the first person or group of people you would tell?

2. The 10 disciples were afraid that they too would be executed as Jesus had. They were hiding behind locked doors fearing for their lives but without a plan of what they should do next. Jesus suddenly appeared without using the doors.

    Finish this statement: Jesus has surprised me by...

3. Do you agree or disagree with the following statement?

    Because Jesus Christ came back from the dead, he is our living hope.

    ❑ I agree
    ❑ I don't know
    ❑ I disagree

4. Jesus' resurrected body still had the wound marks in his hands and side caused by the crucifixion because—

    a) the way you look when you die will be the way you look for all eternity.
    b) they looked really cool.
    c) Christ wanted the disciples and us to be reminded of the price that was paid for our salvation.
    d) the only way to remove them was to die again.

5. What do you think?

    Who needs to hear the good news from you about Christ's love and forgiveness?

    Who needs you to assure them that their sins really are forgiven?

READ OUT LOUD

The 10 disciples were losing hope in the promises of Jesus. Locked away behind (most likely) bolted or barricaded doors, they huddled in fear without a plan for their future. Thinking, perhaps, that the last three years of their lives were wasted on a hoax, they…(well, read it out loud from John 20:18-23).

ASK

What gift do you hope to get for your next birthday?

DISCUSS, BY THE NUMBERS

1. Discuss why your group members picked who they did. And then talk about how they could talk to these selected individuals or groups of people today.
2. Ask, "What do you think was the first thought that popped into the disciples' heads when they saw Jesus?" Share a Jesus surprise story that happened to you.
3. The reality of the resurrection is that Jesus is our living hope. The crucified and risen Christ redeems our past, our present, and our future. Ask, "What does it mean to you that Christ is your living hope?" Read 1 Peter 1:3 out loud.
4. The answer is "c." Jesus' resurrected body still had the wound marks in his hands and side caused by the crucifixion because Christ wanted the disciples (and us) to be reminded of the price he paid for our salvation.
5. Use this item to talk about the importance of (1) telling others about Christ's love and forgiveness and (2) assuring people their sins are forgiven if they turn their lives over to Jesus. Christ talked about both of these in John 20:21, 23.

CLOSE

The resurrected Christ is our living hope—a hope that will never disappoint. Our money and stuff will disappoint. Worldly philosophies will disappoint. Our friendships will disappoint. Even church will disappoint. Christ is the only thing that can give us a living hope that lasts for eternity. Even now Christ is saying to you, "Peace be with you!"

1. How often do you have doubts about God's existence?

☐ All of the time
☐ Some of the time
☐ Hardly ever
☐ Never

2. In your opinion are these statements T (true) or N (not)?

____ Thomas didn't need to meet with the other disciples for his faith to grow.

____ If Thomas had never seen Jesus after the resurrection, he would have abandoned his faith.

____ Thomas' absence from the disciples' meeting where Jesus appeared to them hurt the disciples' growth in Christ as much as it hurt Thomas'.

____ Thomas never showed up to the meeting where the disciples saw Jesus because he had lost faith in Jesus as the Son of God.

____ It was important for Thomas to be with the other disciples, but he blew it off.

____ Thomas ditched the meeting because he thought God had abandoned him when Jesus died.

3. Thomas didn't miss the next meeting of the disciples. He wanted to see Jesus for himself. What are five reasons you shouldn't miss church each week?

#1
#2
#3
#4
#5

4. Stephanie and Marie had been friends for a couple of months. Stephanie had finally gotten up the courage to ask Marie to visit her church.

"You believe in Jesus, right?" asked Stephanie, who figured that if the answer to that question was "no," then she would have to work harder. The answer that Marie gave was a surprise.

"Sure," said Marie. "I believe that Jesus died, everybody dies. But I just don't think that the coming-back-to-life part could be true. That's why I think church is, like, a waste of time to me."

If the resurrection didn't happen, would faith in Christ and going to church be a waste of time?

5. Thomas had to see the resurrected Jesus before declaring him his Savior and Lord. What had to happen for you to decide that Jesus is your Savior and Lord?

☐ I followed at least one of my parents' examples.
☐ I had to realize that my sins stink.
☐ I'm not sure what happened.
☐ Jesus is my Savior (forgave me of my sins) but not my Lord (in charge of my life).
☐ Jesus is not my Savior or my Lord.

But these are written that you may believe that Jesus is the Christ, the Son of God, and that by believing you may have life in his name. (John 20:31, NIV)

READ OUT LOUD
Christ, back from the dead, appeared to 10 of the disciples. Thomas was the only disciple missing at their meeting. And was he in for a surprise. Read the story from John 20:24-31

ASK
What is one amusement park ride that you seriously doubt you will ever try?

DISCUSS, BY THE NUMBERS
1. Doubting is normal. Everyone does it to one degree or another. And doubting is something that can occur throughout life. Some of the disciples doubted Jesus to the end, yet they still believed (Matthew 28:16-17). Doubting is good because it causes you to reflect on what you really believe. It helps you ask questions about your faith in Christ. Encourage your group members to keep coming back and keep asking the hard questions that arise from their doubts.
2. See commentary in bold after each statement.
   - Thomas didn't need to meet with the other disciples for his faith to grow. **Our faith can't grow as well individually as it will in community. That was true of Thomas and is true of us today.**
   - If Thomas had never seen Jesus after the resurrection, he would have abandoned his faith. **Possibly, but most likely he would have come around to believe the eyewitness testimony of the other disciples. Ask, "Can you take it on faith that the disciples, and at least 500 others, witnessed Jesus resurrection?"**
   - Thomas' absence from the disciples' meeting where Jesus appeared to them hurt the disciples' growth in Christ as much as it hurt Thomas. **We really do need each other to grow closer to Jesus. Our Christian growth is best achieved together.**
   - Thomas never showed up to the meeting where the disciples saw Jesus because he had lost faith in Jesus as the Son of God. **It's possible.**

Scripture doesn't give us much to go one with this one. Interesting to debate, though.
   - It was important for Thomas to be with the other disciples, but he blew it off. **Yes. We don't know if he just blew it off, but he certainly needed to be at their gatherings just like we need to meet regularly with our church.**
   - Thomas ditched the meeting because he thought God had abandoned him when Jesus died. **He may very well have felt abandoned and let down because he didn't understand how the crucifixion and death of Jesus could possibly be a good thing.**
3. Thomas didn't miss the next meeting of the disciples. He wanted to see Jesus for himself. What are five reasons you shouldn't miss church each week?
4. As 1 Corinthians 15:17 teaches, our faith is meaningless without the resurrection. Everything we, as Christians, believe hangs on the truth of the resurrection.
5. This is a time to talk with your group about what it means to make Jesus our Savior (forgives our sins) and Lord (in charge of our lives).

But these are written that you may believe that Jesus is the Christ, the Son of God, and that by believing you may have life in his name. (John 20:31, NIV)

CLOSE
The resurrected Christ is our living hope—a hope that will never disappoint. Our money and stuff will disappoint. Worldly philosophies will disappoint. Our friendships will disappoint. Even church will disappoint. Christ is the only thing that can give us a living hope that lasts for eternity. Even now Christ is saying to you, "Peace be with you!"

1. Why do you think Jesus appeared to so many people after his resurrection?

  a) He was collecting the money they owed him.
  b) Jesus wanted to say goodbye to all his friends before he fooled them into thinking he went up into heaven.
  c) He wanted to give his followers proof that the resurrection really happened.
  d) He wanted to show off his appearing/disappearing special effects.
  e) Jesus wanted to show how cool he really was.

2. Finish this sentence stem—

  I think we need the Holy Spirit to help us talk with others about Jesus because...

3. What do you think? Y (yes) or N (no)—

  ___ I have trouble telling others about Jesus.
  ___ I have told at least one other person about Jesus.
  ___ I don't have the gift of telling others about Jesus, so I don't have to.
  ___ My mom or dad tells others about Jesus.
  ___ People will think I'm weird if I talk about Jesus.
  ___ The last time I talked with someone about Jesus, I failed.
  ___ I want to talk with others about Jesus, but I'm too scared.
  ___ I feel guilty for not telling my friends about Jesus.
  ___ I just get into arguments when I talk with others about Jesus.
  ___ I'm not old enough to talk with others about Jesus.
  ___ I don't know enough about the Bible to talk about Jesus with others.
  ___ I share Christ by my actions rather than my words.

4. Do you think it was a miracle the way Jesus went up into heaven?

  ❏ Yes, it was a really cool miracle.
  ❏ No, Jesus fooled the disciples by walking up a mountain into a low-lying cloud.
  ❏ I don't know.

5. In Acts 1:8 Jesus tells us to go all over the world to tell of his love and forgiveness. Below find places that people go to share the gospel. Rate them from places you would be most willing to go (1) to least willing to go (7).

  ___ A place where no one speaks English
  ___ A place where they eat really strange food
  ___ A place that's cold most of the year
  ___ A place where they celebrate different holidays than us
  ___ A place where you know no one
  ___ A place that's hot most of the year
  ___ A place where nearly everyone lives in poverty

 79

READ OUT LOUD

Jesus was ready to exit this world and return to the glory that was his. He gave last-minute instructions to his disciples. Read the story of his exit found in Acts 1:1-11.

ASK

Who is the biggest planner in your family?

DISCUSS, BY THE NUMBERS

1. The answer to the question, "Why do you think Jesus appeared to so many people after his resurrection?" is (c). He wanted to give his followers proof that the resurrection really happened.
2. Listen to your group members' completed sentences. Talk about your church's beliefs about the work of the Holy Spirit in the life of believers.
3. Use this exercise to talk about the good, the bad, and the ugly of evangelism—sharing the gospel with others.
4. Discuss with your group why it was important for the disciples to see one more miracle. The disciples needed to know that Jesus really was God; that his earthly work was done; and that it was now the disciples' responsibility to spread the gospel.
5. Use this activity to see how far out of their comfort zones your group members are willing to go to share Jesus' love and forgiveness with others.

CLOSE

Use the "Jesus (**plus paraphrase**)" reading found in Acts 1:8 to help you close this session.

*But you will receive power (**Listen, you can do this**) when the Holy Spirit (**You don't have to do this on your own**) comes on you; and you will be my witnesses (**You have the privilege of representing Jesus to the world**) in Jerusalem (**within your comfort zone**), and in all Judea and Samaria (**moving out of your comfort zone**), and to the ends of the earth (**way out of your comfort zone**).—Jesus (plus paraphrase), in Acts 1:8 (NIV)*

HOLY FIRE

The Holy Spirit comes at Pentecost

1. **The birthday of the church is marked by the Day of Pentecost. How does your church celebrate Pentecost?**

   ❏ I don't think we do anything.
   ❏ I'm not sure, but we might do something.
   ❏ Our pastor mentions it.
   ❏ We do things to commemorate the day, but I don't pay attention.
   ❏ We make a big deal about the birth of the church.

2. **The disciples were waiting for the giving of the Holy Spirit as Jesus asked them to do. The event was sudden, noisy, attracted attention, and came straight out of heaven. What do you think?**

   ❏ Isn't this just like God to do something spectacular?
   ❏ This is confusing to me.
   ❏ I wish God would do more things like that today.
   ❏ What the disciples experienced was an alien invasion.

3. **What do you think?**

   ❏ I could explain Pentecost to someone in our church.
   ❏ The average person in our church could explain Pentecost to me.

4. **Do you agree or disagree with this statement?**

   The Jews who heard the gospel in their own language and converted to Christianity went back to their home countries and were ashamed of the gospel.

5. **Circle the word that best describes what you think when you hear about the disciples preaching the gospel in different languages.**

   Doubt   Confusion   Excitement   Fear   Disbelief

   Amazement   Joking   Foolishness   Awe   Bewilderment

READ OUT LOUD

Pentecost—also called the Festival of Weeks or the Feast of Harvest—is the Jewish holiday that first commemorated God giving the Ten Commandments to Moses and Israel. Celebrated 50 days after Passover, it was also a time when the Jewish people brought the first fruits of their harvest to the temple. For Christians, it is a celebration of the birth of the church 49 days after Easter (counting Easter gives you 50 days). Read the story of the first Christian Pentecost from Acts 2:1-13.

ASK

What is your favorite kind of birthday cake?

DISCUSS, BY THE NUMBERS

1. However your congregation handles the celebration of Pentecost, it's good for you to have a talk with your group members about the importance of the church. In a world (at least the United States and Canada) that loves individualism, "I" wins out over "We." In this environment the church is often viewed as an organization that must meet my needs rather than the living organism it is—the body of Christ, which worships God and joins him in fulfilling his purposes in this world.

2. Use this as an opportunity to answer your group's questions about the Holy Spirit, speaking in tongues, and Pentecost.

3. Your group members' responses to this activity will give you a good picture of how much your congregation knows about the birth of the church. Use this as a time to talk about the importance of the church in today's world, including why we need each other to grow in our relationship with Jesus.

4. Do you **agree** or **disagree** with this statement?
   Probably most converts, after hearing the gospel preached in their own language, went home and openly shared the gospel. This probably contributed to the rapid spread of Christianity throughout the Roman Empire.

5. Ask, "Would you be willing to learn a different language so that you could share the gospel with those who spoke that language?"

CLOSE

Pentecost marks the birth of the church and serves to remind us that one of our jobs is to share the gospel with others. Different churches have different perspectives about speaking in tongues—something that was done on that first Pentecost—yet we're all part of the universal body of Christ. We share the same purpose—to share the gospel and make disciples of all nations.

PETER TALKS ABOUT JESUS TO THE CROWD

A common strategy for presenting the gospel

1. The 11 apostles stood with the apostle Peter so they could present the gospel together to the crowd. What do you think?

   ❑ I would be more comfortable telling people about Jesus if I were with several other Christians.
   ❑ I would be more comfortable telling people about Jesus if I were with one Christian friend.
   ❑ I would be more comfortable telling people about Jesus if I were by myself.
   ❑ I would be more comfortable not telling people about Jesus.

2. Circle the three words that best describe what Jesus has done for you.

   Purpose   Hope   Forgiveness   Life   Comfort   Peace   Joy

   Strength   Direction   Future   Commitment   Love   Acceptance

3. Peter told the crowd about Jesus' death and resurrection. Which statements are **T (true)** and which are **F (false)?**

   ___ My friends couldn't care less about the death and resurrection of Jesus.
   ___ I don't understand enough about the death and resurrection of Jesus to explain it to those who aren't Christians.
   ___ I'm ready to tell people about Jesus' death and resurrection.
   ___ My friends wouldn't believe me if I told them about Jesus' death and resurrection.
   ___ Pastors are the ones who should tell people about the death and resurrection of Jesus.
   ___ I'm too afraid to talk with people about the death and resurrection of Jesus.

4. Peter talked with the crowd about repentance. I believe repentance means...

   a) telling God you don't want to go to hell.
   b) repeating your sins again and again.
   c) holding your sins inside of you.
   d) telling God you're sorry for your sins.

5. The Bible says about 3,000 people believed. How many people do you think there were who didn't believe?

   ❑ Not very many—less than the 3,000 who believed
   ❑ About 3,000
   ❑ Lots of people

READ OUT LOUD

Peter presents us with what's now a common approach to sharing the gospel of Jesus Christ. First, he explains what is happening. Then, he talks about the death and resurrection of Jesus. Next, he calls the crowd to repentance and baptism. And finally, there are some who believe and some who don't. Read the story found in Acts 2:14-41.

ASK

What's the most excited you ever were after hearing the gospel?

DISCUSS, BY THE NUMBERS

1. The point of this activity—you don't have to share the gospel alone unless you want to. But you do need to share. Address your group members' fears about sharing the gospel with others.

2. The first thing Peter did in presenting the gospel to the crowd was explain what was going on. We can do the same by telling what Jesus has done for us. The circled words are descriptions of what Jesus may have done in the lives of your group members.

3. The second thing Peter did in his gospel presentation was tell of the death and resurrection of Jesus. He said Jesus was sent from God, worked miracles to demonstrate he was God, and died and rose again to prove that he was our Lord and our Savior. Use this item to talk about how to share the death and resurrection of Jesus with others.

4. Use this sentence stem to discuss repentance. The answer is (d) telling God you're sorry for your sins. This passage seems to imply it's the act of baptism that saves us. But we know from other Scriptures that Peter meant adult baptism is our recognition of God's forgiveness of sin. When you're baptized you're declaring that you're sorry for your sins and want the forgiveness Jesus offers.

5. Responses to the gospel typically include many people believing, some worried about the condition of their souls but ultimately not believing, and others flat-out rejecting the gospel message.

CLOSE

Peter gives a simple strategy for sharing the gospel that we may want to try. Talk with others about what Jesus has done in your life and what is happening now. Tell of the death and resurrection of Jesus. Give a chance for the listener to repent. Quote Scripture as Peter did when needed. And finally, give a chance for the listener to believe and be baptized. It's worth a try.

STEPHEN TALKS ABOUT JESUS AND IS KILLED

There are martyrs even today—Christians who die for their faith

1. A Christian martyr is someone who...

a) is made fun of for being a nerd for Jesus.
b) helps old people who are sick.
c) dies for his belief in Jesus Christ.
d) dresses like Old Testament characters.
e) likes to dance to religious songs.

2. Respond to each of these statements with a Y (yes), N (no), or DK (don't know).

___ People don't get martyred in today's world for their belief in Jesus.
___ There are people today who hate Jesus.
___ Everyone in the United States has heard about Jesus already.
___ Christians shouldn't live in places where people don't want to hear about Jesus.
___ Only Jesus freaks get martyred.

3. The Council members were angry at Stephen even though he told them the truth about God. What do you think you should do when people are angry at you because of Jesus?

❑ Ignore them
❑ Laugh at them
❑ Pray for them
❑ Gossip about them
❑ Fight them
❑ Ask why they are afraid
❑ Run
❑ Try talking to them again later
❑ Other: _____

4. At church the pastor asked for prayer for missionaries in danger.

"Why are they in danger?" Joey asked his mom on the way home.

"Because the government officials of some countries where missionaries serve don't want their people to hear about Jesus," said his mom.

"That's crazy," said Joey. "I'm glad we can't get in trouble for talking about Jesus."

How realistic is this story?

5. Answer each of these questions with a Y (yes), N (no), or DK (don't know).

_____ Do you think it was right that Stephen was killed for believing in Jesus?
_____ Do you think it is right that citizens of some Muslim countries are put to death if they convert to Christianity?
_____ Should Christians go to countries as missionaries where they could die for their faith?
_____ Do you think God is mean for letting Christians die because they believe in Jesus?

READ OUT LOUD

Stephen, a deacon of the church in Jerusalem, was the first Christian martyr. He was killed for speaking the truth of the gospel. Some people were upset by what Stephen said, so they made up lies about him (see Acts 6:11-15) in order to get him in trouble with the religious authorities. Stephen was forced to defend himself before the Sanhedrin, the same council that earlier persuaded Pilate to execute Jesus. Read the story in Acts 7:1-60.

ASK

What are Christian beliefs that unbelievers may make fun of?

DISCUSS, BY THE NUMBERS

1. A Christian martyr is someone who... (c) dies for his belief in Jesus Christ
2. See commentary in bold after each statement.
   - People don't get martyred in today's world for their belief in Jesus. **Yes they do. In many countries around the world.**
   - There are people today who hate Jesus. **Yes, and there are different reasons for this. Some people have had hurtful experiences at church. Others may have been told lies about Christianity. So when we talk with people about Jesus, we need to be sensitive to their experiences.**
   - Everyone in the United States has heard about Jesus already. **You would think so, but this isn't true. And many who have heard about Jesus have a distorted picture of him.**
   - Christians shouldn't live in places where people don't want to hear about Jesus. **No, in fact, quite the opposite is true. We need to take the love of Christ everywhere. Perhaps we can't talk to them about Christ but can only show his love. This is still a valuable way of sharing our faith.**
   - Only Jesus freaks get martyred. **True, if you define "Jesus freak" as someone who is outspoken about Jesus.**
3. Listen to your group members' responses. Consider some strategies that might help your group members to act in love toward those who are

angry at them because of their commitment to Jesus.

4. Use this situation to talk further about those places in the world where Christians are still in danger for their beliefs. Create a prayer list of things that need your intervention for these Christians. Take time to pray through your list.
5. See commentary in bold after each statement.
   - Do you think it was right that Stephen was killed for believing in Jesus? **It is never right to murder someone, especially for their religious beliefs.**
   - Do you think it's right that citizens of some Muslim countries are put to death if they convert to Christianity? **Again, putting people to death for religious beliefs, whether Christian or not, is wrong.**
   - Should Christians go to countries as missionaries where they could die for their faith? **Yes, if we believe Jesus loves them and died for them. But Christian missionaries are trained to be careful in how they share Christ and make disciples in these parts of the world so they can avoid bringing harm to anyone.**
   - Do you think God is mean for letting Christians die because they believe in Jesus? **God allows evil because he's given all of us free will to do good or evil. The fallen world we live in became fallen because of a human decision, not God's. God aches to see an end to the pain and suffering our sin creates in the world. But God desires that everyone turn to Jesus.**

CLOSE

Living in a country with religious freedom makes it difficult to understand why there are people who are killed for their faith, Christian or not. But there are. And there always have been since the time of Stephen. What can we do? We can pray. We can support those who go to other countries as missionaries. And maybe, you will become a missionary…

THE CHURCH SPREADS OUT

God wants Christians to spread his love and forgiveness around

1. As Stephen was being brutally killed, he prayed to God, "Lord, do not hold this sin against them" (Acts 7:60). Stephen acted like Christ. I want to...

- ❏ Always act like Christ
- ❏ Most of the time act like Christ
- ❏ Sometimes act like Christ
- ❏ Hardly ever act like Christ
- ❏ Never act like Christ

2. The followers of Christ strongly emphasized the death and resurrection of Jesus. Do you think the church today emphasizes Christ's death and resurrection...

- ❏ Too much
- ❏ About the right amount
- ❏ Not enough

3. Circle the ends of the sentences that apply to you.

When I'm at school—
a) I love talking about Jesus.
b) I sometimes talk about Jesus.
c) I don't talk about Jesus that often.
d) Who's Jesus?

My friends who aren't Christians will—
a) drop me as their friend if I talk with them about Jesus.
b) make fun of me if I talk with them about Jesus.
c) ask me to stop if I talk with them about Jesus.
d) listen if I talk with them about Jesus.

I need to—
a) continue talking about Jesus with my friends who aren't Christians.
b) talk more than I am now with my friends who aren't Christians.
b) figure out what to say about Jesus to my friends who aren't Christians.
d) ask God for courage to talk about Jesus with my friends who aren't Christians.

4. Heidi knew that it would be the right thing to go over and talk to the two girls who were visiting their Sunday school class. She knew they were probably sisters because they looked so much alike. But they also looked sort of, well, plain. Okay…plain, boring, out of style. They definitely were not the type of girls that she normally hung around with at church. What would her friends think? They would think she had lost her mind, that's what they would think. Or worse, they would think that she wanted to hang around them. "They just aren't our type. Don't worry," she could imagine them saying, "they will find someone else to talk to."

How does staying in your own comfortable social group hurt the spread of the gospel?

5. Which is truer? The best way to get Christians excited about Jesus is to—

- ❏ persecute them
- ❏ give them religious liberty

READ OUT LOUD

The church was growing in numbers. A severe persecution broke out in Jerusalem and grew throughout Israel. Stephen was killed because of his faith. Christians scattered throughout the land kept talking about Jesus. Read the story found in Acts 7:54-8:4.

ASK

What does it take to get your group of friends at school to scatter?

DISCUSS, BY THE NUMBERS

Note to Leader: The persecuted Christians in Jerusalem scattered, not because they were persecuted, but because Jesus wanted them to move beyond Jerusalem to share the gospel. We know this because they were persecuted wherever they went, and they still kept sharing the gospel.

1. Stephen's prayer was the prayer Jesus prayed for those who were executing him. Stephen exemplified the character of the Lord. See where your group members are on the scale from "Never act like Christ" to "Always act like Christ." Talk about what it looks like to resemble Jesus when your group members are doing each of the activities listed below:
   • when you're doing chores
   • when you're in a bad mood
   • when you're at the movies
   • while you're surfing the Net
   • while you're at sports practice

2. Use this activity to dialogue with your group about the importance the death and resurrection of Jesus plays in Christianity (REALLY IMPORTANT). Ask, "Do you think our congregation has a healthy perspective on the Christ's death and resurrection?" "Do we place too much emphasis on it?" "Not enough emphasis?"

3. Read Acts 8:4 out loud. Use these statements to talk about the need for us to scatter more and talk about Jesus at school and other locations.

Those who had been scattered preached the word wherever they went. (Acts 8:4, NIV)

4. Read the situation out loud. Use this situation to talk about "scattering" at church to reach all the young people who attend rather than just your small social group.

5. Ask, "Does persecution always light a fire under followers of Christ?" When are times when persecution doesn't work to excite Christians?" "Do we need a severe persecution in the United States and Canada to get Christians sharing the gospel?"

CLOSE

God wants us, as Christ-followers, to spread his love and forgiveness around the world. We can't do this if our world is restricted to a few friends with whom we feel comfortable. So let's get out and spread the gospel.

PHILIP TALKS ABOUT JESUS TO A STRANGER

God puts people in our lives who need to hear the good news

1. **Why do you think it's important for you to share the good news of Jesus' love and forgiveness with your friends who aren't followers of Christ? (You may check more than one box.)**

   ❑ If I don't, nobody else will do it.
   ❑ They are my friends, and I want them to have what I have in Christ.
   ❑ The pastor will be proud of me.
   ❑ I want them to be in heaven with me.
   ❑ My mom will raise my allowance.
   ❑ I will get more points that will help me get into heaven.
   ❑ It's the best news there is.
   ❑ All of my friends already are Christians.
   ❑ Jesus is important to me, and I want him to be important to my friends.
   ❑ I enjoy talking about Jesus with others.

2. **Sherri looked down the long cafeteria table and saw DeAndra. She was eating alone again. She always seemed to be alone.**

   I should talk to her, thought Sherri. *She needs to know that someone cares about her.* Sherri remembered what the pastor had said in church last Sunday—that people who are hurting need to know that Jesus loves them.

   When she saw DeAndra get up, Sherri picked up her tray to follow her. *Okay Lord,* she thought, *give me the words to tell her you love her.*

   If Sherri talks with DeAndra, what do you think will happen?

   • DeAndra may experience God's love and put her faith in Jesus Christ.
   • DeAndra will tell her to get lost.
   • Sherri's school friends will drop her for hanging out with a loser like DeAndra.
   • All the loners at school will start hanging out with Sherri.
   • Sherri will become a loner like DeAndra.
   • DeAndra will end up coming to church with Sherri; Sherri's church friends will dump her for bringing a loner like DeAndra to their church.
   • DeAndra will put her faith in Christ and tell others about Jesus.

3. **Name three people you know who aren't Christians you would be willing to talk with about Christ if you received ideas on how to do so.**

   #1 _____

   #2 _____

   #3 _____

4. **Circle *one* of the following five Bible verses you could use to talk with someone about Jesus.**

   John 3:17   John 10:10   Romans 3:23   Romans 6:23   Ephesians 2:8-9

5. **Write *agree* or *disagree* for each of these statements.**

   _____ a) Christian young people need to share their faith in Christ less often.
   _____ b) It is a Christian's responsibility to make others put their faith in Jesus.
   _____ c) It's easy to tell your friends about Jesus.
   _____ d) Most young people in the United States are already Christians.
   _____ e) Christians shouldn't push Jesus on those who don't believe.

READ OUT LOUD

In today's story, Philip was nudged by an angel of the Lord to head in a new direction. God intended to keep the gospel moving from Jerusalem and Judea to Samaria and then to the whole earth (see the words of Jesus in Acts 1:8). Philip was used by God to spread the gospel to Africa through an important Ethiopian official who had converted to Judaism. You can read the story of Philip and the Ethiopian in Acts 8:26-40.

ASK

Which of your friends do you find it easiest to talk with?

DISCUSS, BY THE NUMBERS

1. A statistic that's been thrown around for years in youth ministry in the United States (and validated by empirical research) is that 85 percent of those who make a commitment to Christ do so before the age of 14. This means that there is an exciting window of opportunity for young people in middle school/junior high to share their faith with friends. Go over these statements to look at the best reasons for your group members to share their faith.

2. Ask your group members to talk about the choices they picked. Use this as a time to talk about the risks we take when we share Jesus with others.

3. Count how many people your group members listed. Then use this time to brainstorm with your group strategies for talking about Jesus with them.

4. With your group members, talk about each of the Bible passages—specifically how the verse could be used to talk about Jesus with friends.

5. See commentary in bold after each statement.
   • Christian young people need to share their faith in Christ less often. **Most young people, like adults, need to talk about Jesus more often rather than less often.**
   • It is a Christian's responsibility to make others put their faith in Jesus. **No, the Bible teaches that it's our responsibility to share Christ (Matthew 28:19) and the Holy Spirit's responsibility to convict of sin (John 16:8).**
   • It's easy to tell your friends about Jesus. **Sometimes yes, sometimes no.**
   • Most young people in the United States are already Christians. **No. About half go to church sometime during a given month.**
   • Christians shouldn't push Jesus on those who don't believe. **Debate with your group—is talking about Jesus or sharing the gospel "pushing Jesus"?**

CLOSE

Just as God put the Ethiopian stranger in Philip's life, God puts people in our lives who need to hear the good news. There are many in my life that I haven't talked with about Jesus, just as there are in your life. We often let fear stand in the way of telling others about Jesus. While there are times we shouldn't share Jesus with someone, there are many more times when we should but we don't. Let's commit together to talk with one person this week about Jesus.

NO PLAYING FAVORITES

Christ treats everyone the same

1. My home is...

- like Cornelius' because we are all followers of Christ.
- mostly like Cornelius' because most of my family follows Christ.
- sort of like Cornelius' because some of my family members follow Christ.
- unlike Cornelius' because I'm the only Christ-follower.

2. Answer each of these questions as best you can.

- Which group at your school is the coolest?

- Which group at your school is the weirdest?

- Which group at your school is the dumbest?

- Which group at your school is the luckiest?

- Which group at your school is your favorite?

- Which group at your school is God's favorite?

3. "Ugh," said Devon as she fanned her face. She and her mother were standing on the corner waiting for the light to turn green. Next to them was a homeless woman. It was a warm day and it was pretty obvious to Devon, who was standing next to her, that she hadn't taken a bath in quite a while.

"Don't be rude, Devon," whispered her mother. "God loves her as much as he loves you."

Right, thought Devon, *God doesn't have to smell her*.

What do you think Devon should do?

4. Put a check next to those statements that you believe are true.

_____ You are accepted by God if the good you do outweighs the bad.
_____ The United States is a Christian nation favored by God.
_____ God cares more for the rich than the poor.
_____ Homosexuals will never be accepted by God.
_____ Jesus has a tough time loving drug addicts.
_____ New Orleans was devastated by a Level 5 hurricane because of sinfulness.
_____ God sent the 9/11 terrorists to hell.
_____ The Lord forgives anyone who asks.
_____ God doesn't care about skin color.
_____ The Lord accepts everyone into heaven.

5. How do you think Peter did in presenting the gospel to Cornelius and his family? Has your family heard about the love and forgiveness Jesus offers? Why do you think Peter talked about the death and resurrection of Jesus every time he shared the gospel with people?

READ OUT LOUD

Cornelius was not Jewish but did worship the God of the Bible. He had passed his faith on to all who lived in his home—family and servants. Evidence of his relationship with God can be seen in both his prayer life and in his charity to the poor. He had a vision that you can read in the story from Acts 10:23-48.

ASK

What is your favorite ice cream flavor?

DISCUSS, BY THE NUMBERS

1. This item gives you a great opportunity to discuss the faith of group members' families without putting anyone, especially moms and dads, down.

2. These questions help your group members see that, while they treat people differently, God treats people the same. And we should want all of these groups of people to know Jesus.

   Then Peter began to speak: "I now realize how true it is that God does not show favoritism but accepts men from every nation who fear him and do what is right." (Acts 10:34, NIV)

3. Read the situation out loud. Use it to talk about God's desire to reach out to everyone with the love of Christ, including those who are socially disenfranchised.

4. See commentary in bold after each statement.

   • You are accepted by God if the good you do outweighs the bad. **No, we can never do enough good to be made acceptable before God.**

   • The United States is a Christian nation favored by God. **This is an interesting one to debate. Explore the notion of a Christian nation. Can we really call the U.S. a Christian nation? Regardless of the answers discussed by your group, remind them that God does not play favorites among the nations. Grace and salvation is offered to all.**

   • God cares more for the rich than the poor. **God cares for everyone. God does, however, want us to help the poor.**

   • Homosexuals will never be accepted by God. **Not true. If they have repented and accepted** the forgiveness offered to them by Christ, then they are just as accepted by God as any other Christian.

   • Jesus has a tough time loving drug addicts. **No, but we may have a tough time. Remember, Jesus says we must love even those who are difficult to love.**

   • New Orleans was devastated by a Level 5 hurricane because of sinfulness. **No, New Orleans was devastated because it happened to be in the path of the hurricane. If God decided to destroy places because of sin, your community would be devastated also.**

   • God sent the 9/11 terrorists to hell. **No. People who end up in hell send themselves there by rejecting Jesus.**

   • The Lord forgives anyone who asks. **Yes, that's why he died and rose again.**

   • God doesn't care about skin color. **Yes. All people are equal before God.**

   • The Lord accepts everyone into heaven. **No, only those who are forgiven of their sins.**

5. Work through each of the questions as a group. **These questions help you dialogue with your group about the necessity of the death and resurrection of Jesus. There is no other way to salvation. If there were, God would have done it and spared Jesus the pain and suffering.**

CLOSE

Isn't it wonderful that God doesn't play favorites? If God favored some of us over others, we might be the ones not headed for heaven. And because God doesn't play favorites, we can't, either. We need to share God's love with everyone. We need to talk about Christ with everyone.

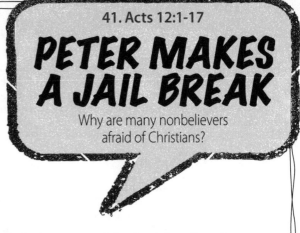

PETER MAKES A JAIL BREAK

Why are many nonbelievers afraid of Christians?

1. **Why do you think God permitted Herod Agrippa to kill James, one of Jesus' first disciples?**

   • Because God is mean
   • So that the other believers in Jerusalem would get out of Jerusalem and spread the gospel
   • To show that a time of persecution was coming
   • God allowed it to happen but didn't cause it to happen
   • We won't know until we get to heaven
   • Because God wanted believers to see that they didn't need the original disciples any longer
   • To punish James for his sins

2. **Herod Agrippa arrested and killed followers of Christ. Circle the one word that best describes the persecution Christians suffer for their faith in the United States and Canada. Underline the one word that best describes the persecution Christians suffer for their faith in some Muslim countries.**

   Compassion   Annoyance   Oppression   Torture   Barbarism

   Harassment   Murder   Kindness   Teasing   Torment

3. **The Christians at Mary's house were surprised to see Peter out of jail even though they were praying for him. Are you surprised when God answers your prayers with a "Yes"?**

   • I am always surprised
   • I am usually surprised
   • I am sometimes surprised
   • I am never surprised

   Why?

4. **Do you A (agree) or D (disagree)?**

   ___ a) Like Peter, I'm harassed for being a Christian.
   ___ b) I don't tell people at my school or on my sports team that I am a follower of Christ.
   ___ c) People today think it's uncool to be a Christian.
   ___ d) I'm not brave enough to stand up for my Christian faith like James or Peter.
   ___ e) Persecution of Christians scares me.

5. **Mark these statements true or false—**

   • People who haven't put their faith in Jesus are afraid of Christians. _____
   • In some countries where Islam is the dominant religion, it's illegal to convert to Christianity. That's because Muslims fear Christianity. _____
   • Atheists—those who don't believe in God—make fun of Christians because they wish they had the joy experienced by Christians. _____
   • Christians are persecuted because it makes nonbelievers feel like they're wrong in their beliefs. _____
   • Christians should harass people who haven't put their faith in Christ. _____

READ OUT LOUD

Herod Agrippa loved popularity, and the persecution of the church made him popular with his citizens. Rather than seek justice and do the right thing, he did what pleased the people he ruled. You can read the story from Acts 12:1-17.

ASK

When are you the most afraid?

DISCUSS, BY THE NUMBERS

1. See commentary in bold after each statement.
   - because God is mean. **Just the opposite. God is loving and merciful and has granted humanity free will. Humans take that free will and often use it for evil purposes. Yet God's love and power overcome all evil in the world. God can use anything that happens in our lives to further his just, holy, and good purposes.**
   - so that the other believers in Jerusalem would get out of Jerusalem and spread the gospel. **Jesus had commanded his disciples (Acts 1:8) to share the gospel in Jerusalem, then Judea and Samaria, and then throughout the world. But the disciples and new converts were huddled in Jerusalem, unwilling to venture out.**
   - to show that a time of persecution was coming. **The persecution did continue to increase. Perhaps seeing the execution of James, and the persecution of Peter, showed the new followers of Jesus that they too may have to suffer for their faith.**
   - God allowed it to happen but didn't cause it to happen. **God does allow evil things to happen without causing them to happen. This is God's permissive will whereby he uses bad circumstances for good (Romans 8:28).**
   - we won't know until we get to heaven. **What we see and know now is distorted, like looking into a fogged-up mirror (1 Corinthians 13:12). In heaven we will get a clearer picture.**
   - because God wanted believers to see that they didn't need the original disciples any longer. **The early converts did depend upon the disciples who had been with Jesus for encouragement and teaching. God knew that the time would soon come when the disciples would be out of the picture. The death of James could have been preparing them for future leadership.**
   - to punish James for his sins. **God would not have punished James for his sins because those sins were forgiven at the cross.**
2. The persecution faced by today's Christians in the United States and Canada is nothing compared to that experienced by the early Christians, as well as Christians in some Muslim countries. Ask, "What is the good in not being persecuted for your Christian faith?" and "What is the downside of not being persecuted?"
3. Ask for a show of hands for the most popular answer.

Tell a story from your life when you were surprised at God's quick "Yes" to your prayers. Ask, "Why do you think we are so often surprised by God's answers to our prayers?" "Do you expect God to answer your prayers?"

4. See commentary in bold after each statement.
   a) Like Peter, I'm harassed for being a Christian. **Ask, "Have you ever been hassled or made fun of for your beliefs?"**
   b) I don't tell people at my school or on my sports team that I am a follower of Christ's. **Ask, "How do people at your school know that you are a Christ-follower?"**
   c) People today think it's uncool to be a Christian. **Some do while others don't. Ask, "Who are the people who think it's uncool?" "Are there some people who are neutral?"**
   d) I'm not brave enough to stand up for my Christian faith like James or Peter. **Ask, "Do you think God will give you the strength to endure whatever circumstance you'll face in the future?" "Do you sense the presence of Christ in your life now?"**
   e) Persecution of Christians scares me. **Ask, "Why might persecution scare you?" "How often do you think about persecuted Christians in other countries?"**
5. See commentary in bold after each statement.
   - People who haven't put their faith in Jesus are afraid of Christians. **Some are while some aren't. Use this statement as an opportunity to talk about why people are afraid of Christians.**
   - In some countries where Islam is the dominant religion, it's illegal to convert to Christianity. **Discuss why Muslim leaders in Muslim countries might not want their people converting to Christianity. Are they just afraid of Christianity, or might they have other reasons?**
   - Atheists—those who don't believe in God—make fun of Christians because they wish they had the joy experienced by Christians. **Good statement to debate. Do atheists lack the joy that comes from Jesus?**
   - Christians are persecuted because it makes nonbelievers feel like they're right in their beliefs. **This is often the case. Persecution makes the persecutor feel superior.**
   - Christians should harass people who haven't put their faith in Christ. **Of course not. Christians should be understanding, even when someone refuses Christ. Jesus loved people, healed, and fed them, even when they weren't believers.**

CLOSE

The persecution of the early church demonstrates the fear people had of Christians. Jesus was present with these early Christians who faced the fear and anger of those who did not believe. As a result, the greater the persecution, the greater the growth and boldness of the church! The Christian faith continued to spread despite the fears of non-believers and their subsequent attempts to wipe it out. Today, Christianity continues to spread, growing rapidly in Central and South America, Africa, and Asia.

HEROD PLAYS GOD

God is God—and you're not

1. Are you in control or not in control of each of the following?

	Totally in Control	Kinda in Control	Not in Control
• The time you wake up	❑	❑	❑
• If you do your homework	❑	❑	❑
• If the school bus gets into an accident	❑	❑	❑
• What your dad does with his money	❑	❑	❑
• The weather	❑	❑	❑
• Who will be your school's next principal	❑	❑	❑
• What you eat for breakfast	❑	❑	❑

2. What is truer? I act like I'm God when—

❑ I worry about the future.
❑ I turn my worries about the future over to God.

3. Finish this sentence.

Our culture treats celebrities like gods because—

4. Why doesn't God strike down everyone who acts (like Herod) with such royal self-importance?

a) There aren't that many people who act as though they are God.
b) He doesn't want to make Christians angry.
c) Because we would all be dead.
d) God likes to watch people get hurt.

5. Read this short story, then you can discuss it with your group.

Candace was always getting new clothes. This fact made her the envy of many of the girls in eighth grade. She had new shoes, purses, coats—just about anything in the latest style you could think of. When she walked down the halls, the girls just stopped and stared with their mouths open.

"Can you believe that outfit?" Belinda asked her friend Anna. "I think I just saw that in a magazine."

"It must have cost a fortune," whispered Anna to Belinda as Candace walked toward them.

"Hey Candace," they both said.

"Hey," said Candace in return.

"I like your outfit," said Belinda.

"Yeah," said Anna. "That would look really cute with that leather coat you wore last week."

"Oh, that," said Candace in a bored voice that made the other girls crazy. "I lost it over the weekend."

"You lost it!" Anna said, a little too loudly. "You parents must have been ready to kill you."

"No. It didn't seem to bother them. My mom said I could get a new one if I wanted to," said Candace as she turned to walk into class.

Anna and Belinda, mouths open, just looked at each other.

"That coat cost more than my entire wardrobe, I bet," said Belinda.

"Yours and mine both. Come on," said Anna as she pulled her friend into the classroom.

6. Why do you think the good news about Jesus kept spreading so quickly?

But the word of God continued to increase and spread. (Acts 12:24)

READ OUT LOUD

Herod arrogantly killed James, one of the 12 disciples. Seeing that the people liked the execution of a Christian, he arrested Peter so he, too, could be killed. But Peter was led away from jail during the night by an angel. The soldiers guarding Peter were worried when they couldn't find Peter. You can read the story from Acts 12:18-24.

ASK

How do people at your school treat those who think too much of themselves?

DISCUSS, BY THE NUMBERS

1. We often live with the illusion that we are in total control of our lives. This activity is designed to get your group members thinking about some of the ways we don't have control—and to remind us of our need to trust in God.

2. Worrying is like playing God. Here are seven reasons why.

- You think you have control of the situation about which you are worrying.
- Worrying is a sign that you trust in yourself rather than almighty God.
- You worry like somehow that has the power to change things.
- Worrying puts you at the center of your universe.
- Worrying gives you an illusion that you're in control of the situation.
- You take over God's role even though he is in charge of your life.
- You make yourself out to be the Creator rather than the creation.

3. Listen to the completed sentences. Then talk about all the "whys" and the "ways" we treat celebrities like gods. Ask, "How does treating celebrities like gods hurt them?" "Hurt us?"

4. The answer is (c) Because we would all be dead. We are so self-centered that we don't even realize it. Ask your group members to go through their day, identifying how often they considered themselves without considering the interests of others.

5. This situation is an example of how people can assume the role of a god. Answer these questions with your group, "Which of these people are assuming the role of a god? Why do you think so?" "Could this situation have really happened?" "How often do you see this kind of behavior at your school? At your church? In your after-school activities?"

6. Discuss the reasons your group members believe God's message kept spreading so quickly.

CLOSE

Herod became arrogant—so conceited that he thought he was more a god than a human. And we can fall into the same trap if we aren't careful. Remember, God is God—and you're not. So let God be God, the Creator. As his creation, let's trust in him to take care of us.

1. **How committed was the apostle Paul to Jesus?**

   ❑ Slightly committed to Jesus
   ❑ 50 percent committed to Jesus
   ❑ Totally sold out to Jesus

43. Acts 19:23-34

THE MAIN THING

What is most important?

2. **Which out of the following list is most important to you?**

   ❑ Getting into trouble   ❑ Having fun
   ❑ Being first   ❑ Looking good
   ❑ Trusting in Jesus   ❑ Acting cool
   ❑ Being tough

3. **If you were asked why Jesus is so important in your life, how would you respond?**

4. **Sarah's friend Ella really wanted Sarah to spend the night. They had been talking about it for weeks. Ella had a bunch of great stuff that she wanted them to do together.**

   "So you can come over Saturday?" asked Ella.

   "Oh, Ella," said Sarah, "couldn't it be Friday night?"

   "No," said Ella. "My mom said that it had to be Saturday. Why?"

   "It's just that I go to church on Sunday morning," said Sarah.

   "Ugh!" Ella said. "Couldn't you just miss this once? It's just church."

   Sarah thought about it for a minute. Lately it seemed that she had really started to enjoy church. She liked the music and had started really listening to the sermon. She had even started reading the Bible on her own. Jesus had become real to her. She would miss hearing about him.

   "No," said Sarah, "I don't think I want to miss church. Maybe you can come over to my house on Friday night."

   Have you come to the conclusion that Jesus is the main thing? What happened to convince you of this truth?

5. **I can keep Jesus the main thing in my life by—**

   • Getting involved in a small group Bible study
   • Keeping connected to Christian friends
   • Serving others
   • Ignoring my parents
   • Talking often about Jesus
   • Trying alcohol
   • Staying committed to worship at church
   • Praying often
   • Blowing off school
   • Reading a Bible devotion every day

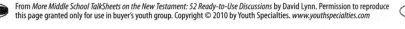

READ OUT LOUD

Paul traveled to Ephesus during his third missionary trip. There he found many opportunities to strengthen the few believers already living in Ephesus and to preach the gospel. Many people became followers of Christ (called *The Way*) in Ephesus. Other names were *The Lord's Way* or *God's Way*. As usual, there was opposition. Read the rest of the story found in Acts 19:23-34.

ASK

How committed are you to your favorite TV program?

DISCUSS, BY THE NUMBERS

1. Ask, "What did Paul do as a result of his dedication to Jesus? What changes have you seen in your life as you've become more dedicated to Jesus?"
2. Explore the top three. Talk about what this list would look like for a committed Christian. How about a nominal Christian?
3. Role-play this question. Ask a group member to volunteer to stand up. Ask, "If you were asked why Jesus is so important in your life, how would you respond?"
4. Talk about what circumstances led you, and then your group members, to the conclusion that Jesus is the main thing.
5. Talk about the activities that can help and hinder keeping Jesus the main thing in our lives.

CLOSE

The most important thing in our lives is Jesus. Yet, keeping Jesus as our main focus is often difficult. Christians have always used simple practices to keep Jesus front and center. These include: Regular participation in church worship, daily prayer and Bible reading, faith conversations with other Christians, time in fellowship with other believers, service to others, and other spiritual disciplines.

GET GUARDED

Be alert to those who want to deceive you

1. **Paul felt he had taught the church everything God wanted them to know in order to live for Jesus. Which of the following statements is true for you?**

❑ I have learned everything that God wants me to know to live for Jesus.
❑ I have learned almost everything that God wants me to know to live for Jesus.
❑ I have learned some of the things that God wants me to know to live for Jesus.
❑ I have learned a couple of the things that God wants me to know to live for Jesus.
❑ I have learned nothing that God wants me to know to live for Jesus.

For I have not hesitated to proclaim to you the whole will of God.
(Acts 20:27, NIV)

2. **"Aw Mom, just ten more minutes," grumbled Matt as his mom tried to wake him up. It was Sunday morning, and, as usual, he wasn't the cheeriest person when he woke up.**

"Get up, Matt, we need to leave in twenty minutes so you can be there to welcome. It's your week, remember," said his mom as she opened the blinds in his room.

Great, thought Matt. Why did I ever think that it would be fun to be on the Welcoming Team? Mr. Cox had made it sound like they had a special job in the church. What they really had to do was get up earlier than usual for church. It was kind of fun to be part of the team, he guessed.

"Okay, okay, I'm up already," he said as he threw his covers back and got out of bed.

Paul told the Ephesian church leaders to watch after themselves and others in the church. How is Matt doing this? How is Matt not doing this? How are you doing this? How are you not doing this?

Keep watch over yourselves and all the flock of which the Holy Spirit has made you overseers.
Be shepherds of the church of God, which he bought with his own blood. (Acts 20:28, NIV)

3. **Mark each answer with a + (yes), - (no) or ? (maybe).**

____ TV preachers are the "savage wolves" Paul talked about.
____ The church is full of hypocrites.
____ Paul's warning to be on guard against those who want to deceive Christians is no longer needed today.
____ The fighting and dissension that goes on in the church today also happened in Paul's day.
____ Like Paul, I have been attacked by people who don't like Jesus.

So be on your guard! Remember that for three years I never stopped
warning each of you night and day with tears. (Acts 20:31, NIV)

4. **Check the one that makes the most sense to you.**
   God's wonderful kindness and mercy help me live each day—

❑ and get away with sinning and doing whatever I want.
❑ to rely on myself.
❑ to live a holy life, free from being a slave to sin.
❑ by trying really hard to do better.

Now I commit you to God and to the word of his grace, which can build you up and give you an inheritance
among all those who are sanctified. (Acts 20:32, NIV)

5. **Paul asked that the church help the weak. Circle the one group that you think needs the most help today.**

Poor	Homeless	Mentally Challenged	Hungry	Orphans
Disabled	Alcoholics	Abused	Jobless	Drug Addicts	Refugees

READ OUT LOUD

Paul is saying goodbye to his Christian friends. He's been called by the Holy Spirit to go to Jerusalem. He knows he probably will never see them again. He gives them parting advice, prays with them, and… you can read the story found in Acts 20:13-38.

ASK

Who is the easiest person you know to play a trick on?

DISCUSS, BY THE NUMBERS

1. Use this activity to discuss what your group members still need to learn and how they can learn it. Also, connect this to Paul's warning to guard against false teachings. Ask, "How can learning more about God and the Bible help us guard against deception?"

2. Read Acts 20:28 out loud. Use these questions to talk about the responsibility we have for watching out for ourselves and those God wants us to care for in our church. Matt is doing this by being part of the welcoming team. He is shirking his responsibility, though, when he doesn't want to get up earlier than normal.

   Keep watch over yourselves and all the flock of which the Holy Spirit has made you overseers. Be shepherds of the church of God, which he bought with his own blood. (Acts 20:28, NIV)

3. See commentary in bold after each statement.
   - TV preachers are the "savage wolves" Paul talked about. **There are dangerous teachers in today's church, just as there were in Paul's day. Some TV preachers are and some aren't.**
   - The church is full of hypocrites. **Yes. And each of us is one. That's why we need to keep going to church.**
   - Paul's warning to be on guard against those who want to deceive Christians is no longer needed today. **No. There are many people, inside and outside the church, who are deceiving Christians with false doctrines. This is especially true with the amount of New Age teaching making the rounds on TV and in books.**
   - The fighting and dissension that goes on in the church today also happened in Paul's day. **Yes. It's in everyone's church. Our job is to be like Jesus in the middle of this dissension.**

- Like Paul, I have been attacked by people who don't like Jesus. **Some time in every committed Christian's life, there will be attacks from those who don't understand or respect your commitment to Jesus.**

So be on your guard! Remember that for three years I never stopped warning each of you night and day with tears. (Acts 20:31, NIV)

4. Check the one that makes the most sense to you. God's wonderful kindness and mercy helps me live each day—
   - ❏ and get away with sinning and doing whatever I want. **No, grace means you are freed *from* sin not *to* sin**
   - ❏ to rely on myself. **Grace gives you the chance to rely on God, the only one who can help you live the Christian life.**
   - ❏ to live a holy life, free from being a slave to sin. **Yes, your sins are forgiven and now you are freed from the slavery of sin and free to live a holy life. You can also know that you are forgiven when you blow it.**
   - ❏ by trying really hard to do better. **No way. Living on our own power does nothing but frustrate us.**

Now I commit to God and to the word of his grace, which can build you up and give you an inheritance among all those who are sanctified. (Acts 20:32, NIV)

5. Throughout the Bible we are commanded to help the poor, the homeless, the orphan, the widow, and more. Ask, "Why is it so easy for us to forget this command?"

Note: Paul tells us that Jesus said, "It is more blessed to give than to receive" (Acts 20:35, CEV). Jesus said this, but it's not recorded in the Gospels. We must rely on Paul to tell us the words of Jesus. It certainly sounds like something that could have been in the Gospels.

CLOSE

Paul's warning to guard ourselves against lies and deception is as true today as it was in his day. Let's continue to pray and learn all we can about the Bible, so we can remain faithful to Jesus and steer clear of the world's deceptions.

THE SIX-HOUR SERMON

Taking the time to "talk" Jesus
with other Christians

**1. Everywhere he went Paul encouraged those who
followed Christ. What encourages you the most?**

- ❏ Worship with other Christians
- ❏ Eating a meal with other followers of Christ
- ❏ Partying with other Christians
- ❏ Bible study by myself
- ❏ Prayer and Bible reading with others
- ❏ Youth group
- ❏ Service projects with others from my church
- ❏ Other: _____

**2. Paul was a special guest speaker of the church in Troas.
Do you like special guest speakers at your church worship service
or the regular teacher/pastor who speaks?**

- ❏ I like special guest speakers
- ❏ I like our regular teacher/pastor who speaks
- ❏ I like a little of both
- ❏ I don't like either

**3. Paul mixed preaching with discussion when he taught the congregation in Troas.
Check the following boxes if you've ever—**

- ❏ talked with others about a sermon preached in your church.
- ❏ participated with other youth in an adult Sunday school class discussion.
- ❏ co-led a faith discussion with an adult.
- ❏ taken part in a multi-generational Bible study.

4. Like Eutychus, have you ever fallen asleep during a sermon or faith discussion at your church?

- ❏ YES
- ❏ NO

**5. Eutychus was brought back to life by Paul. What events within your congregation give
you the most life?**

- ❏ Sunday school
- ❏ Small group Bible study
- ❏ Worship
- ❏ Service events
- ❏ One-on-one time with another Christian
- ❏ Prayer services
- ❏ Youth group
- ❏ Retreats/camps
- ❏ Other: _____

READ OUT LOUD

Sunday, for Christians, had taken the place of Saturday, the Jewish Sabbath. Sunday was a day to remember Christ's resurrection. And in the early church, Communion, the Lord's Supper, which is sometimes called the Eucharist, was celebrated each Sunday. Paul came to the church in Troas to celebrate the Lord's Supper with them on that Sunday. He also taught and discussed faith issues all night. You can read the story from Acts 20:1-12.

ASK

Who is the last person you text before you go to bed and the first person you text when you get up in the morning?

DISCUSS, BY THE NUMBERS

1. Today's story opens with Paul encouraging other followers of Christ. Find out what encourages your group members the most and why.
2. Explore what your group members like the most and why. Talk about why it can be good to have a guest speaker now and then to get a new perspective. Like Paul coming to town, a guest speaker or teacher can help energize your faith. Media presentations or in-person speakers are a good way to keep learning more about our faith.
3. This item explores how often your group members get to dialogue about their faith. Ask, "Why is it important for us to have faith conversations rather than just listen to a speaker preach?" If your group members aren't used to discussing faith issues, they may have a harder time getting into conversations about Jesus. All the more reason to take opportunities to encourage faith conversations among your group.
4. Have some fun telling "nodding off" stories.
5. Explore with your group members which activities energize their faith the most. If time permits, talk about one activity they'd like to see done again, and why they found it most effective.

CLOSE

In today's busy world, it seems as though we have no extended time to talk about Jesus with other Christians. It is imperative we make time—big chunks of time—for faith conversations. Like those Christians in the early church, we too need time to think and reflect on what it means to follow Christ.

PAUL REVIEWS HIS JESUS STORY

Reflecting on our lives can motivate us to move forward for Jesus

1. Paul liked to talk to people about Jesus, whether one person or a crowd. In today's story he preaches to an angry mob. Why do you think he took advantage of every opportunity to share the good news of Jesus' love and forgiveness?

   ❏ He made money from every soul he preached to.
   ❏ He wanted to give as many people as possible the opportunity for salvation.
   ❏ He liked to argue and make people mad at Jesus.
   ❏ He had issues from his childhood.
   ❏ He knew hell was a real place.
   ❏ He loved God and his neighbor.
   ❏ He took the Great Commission seriously (Matthew 28:18-20).

2. "She's really changed, Mom," said Polly. Polly was talking about her friend Jill.

   "She has changed a lot since you invited her to church," agreed Polly's mom.

   "She doesn't swear as much and she even reads her Bible now. She's really becoming a stronger Christian," said Polly.

   "And what about you, young lady?" said her mom. "Who would have thought that you would have the courage to ask Jill to church? That would have never happened last year."

   Polly considered this for a moment before answering. "You're right," she said. "I guess I have grown, too."

   Why do you think Jesus changes you whether you grew up knowing him or just met him?

3. Paul gave his life story to the angry mob so they could hear what Jesus had done for him. Use these statements to review your life with Jesus. Circle the answer that best fits you in the following three situations.

   During this past year I have—
   a) grown closer to Jesus
   b) stayed the same with Jesus
   c) moved further away from Jesus

   I became a Christian when—
   a) I can't remember, I was so young
   b) recently
   c) in the last few years

   I'm glad I have faith in Jesus because—
   a) he is my Lord and Savior
   b) I don't like any of the other religions
   c) it gets my parents off my back

4. Is your life different, because of Christ, from the lives of people you know who don't follow him?

   ❏ I must confess that my life is not different from those who don't follow Jesus.
   ❏ My life is a little different but not much.
   ❏ My life is becoming more and more different each week.
   ❏ My life is dramatically different.

5. *"Then the Lord said to [Paul], 'Go; I will send you far away to the Gentiles'"* (**Acts 22:21, NIV**). **Finish this sentence stem.**

   God wants me to—

READ OUT LOUD

The apostle Paul wrapped up his third missionary trip. Agabus, a prophet of God, accurately predicted Paul's persecution that awaited him in Jerusalem. The followers of Christ who were with Paul begged him not to return to Jerusalem. Paul refused, telling them he was ready to go to jail or even die for Jesus. Back in Jerusalem a crowd attacked him for being a Jesus follower. So Paul was carried to a Roman fortress for his own safety. There he asked if he could speak to the wild mob. Pick up the story from here and read it aloud from Acts 22:1-21.

ASK

What is the best way for you to review spelling words?

DISCUSS, BY THE NUMBERS

1. See commentary in bold after each statement.
- He made money from every soul he preached to. **No money was made. In fact, Paul worked as a tentmaker while he preached.**
- He wanted to give as many people as possible the opportunity for salvation. **Just like God, Paul wanted to see salvation come to as many as possible.**
- He liked to argue and make people mad at Jesus. **No, but he sometimes did make people mad—those who rejected Jesus.**
- He had issues from his childhood. **He may have, but if he did this wasn't his motivation for sharing Jesus with everyone he could.**
- He knew hell was a real place. **Yes, he believed that the doctrine of hell was true.**
- He loved God and his neighbor. **Yes, which gave him his motivation.**
- He took the Great Commission seriously (Matthew 28:18-20). **Yes, he did. You can read the Great Commission from Matthew 28:18-20.**
2. Jesus changed Jill, a recent convert to Christ. You will have group members who grew up in Christian homes and those who only recently were introduced to Jesus. The Lord changes both. Use this story as a springboard to discuss the question, "Why do you think Jesus changes you whether you grew up knowing him or just met him?"
3. Use these three sentence stems to review your and your group members' relationships with Christ. Ask, "How can reviewing your relationship with Jesus motivate you to move forward with him?"
4. Go over each statement, asking "why" after each one. Tell your group members to please be honest. This is an open and critical look at our lives. You go first in sharing.
   - ❑ I must confess that my life is not different from those who don't follow Jesus.
   - ❑ My life is a little different but not much.
   - ❑ My life is becoming more and more different each week.
   - ❑ My life is dramatically different.
5. Point out that no matter where we go or what we do, we can be a witness, like Paul, for Jesus Christ.

CLOSE

Paul reviewed his life both before and after he met Jesus. His did this in order to show how his life had been changed by his encounter with Christ. We can review our lives and relationships with Jesus to help motivate us to move forward with Jesus.

PAUL ACTS CHRISTIAN

Christians who are treated unfairly
act differently than nonbelievers

1. Paul was treated unfairly. Paul was put in prison wrongfully. Paul was kept in prison unlawfully. And yet he acted differently as a Christian than those who didn't follow Christ, like Governor Felix or Ananias, the high priest. Check the ways Paul acted that reflected Jesus.

   - ❏ Paul stayed calm in the midst of the raging of those who accused him.
   - ❏ Paul secretly hated his accusers.
   - ❏ Paul didn't get an attitude like his accusers.
   - ❏ Paul paid a hit man to kill Ananias, the high priest.
   - ❏ Paul didn't bribe when Felix wanted a bribe.
   - ❏ Paul told the truth while his accusers lied.
   - ❏ Paul refused to talk badly about those who accused him while they trash-talked him.
   - ❏ Paul gossiped about his accusers while in jail.

2. Governor Felix knew quite a lot about The Way. That's what Christianity was called at the time of Paul. What other names do you think would be cool to call Christianity?

3. Felix knew all about Christianity or The Way. What Christianity taught about how to live and the coming judgment scared him. But he didn't say he was sorry for his sins. And he kept putting off the decision to become a follower of Christ. Why was that a bad idea? Do you know anyone who keeps putting off this most important decision?

4. As the guard entered the cell and gave Paul his food he just stopped and stared. "How do you do it?" he asks.

   "You mean eat the food?" Paul answers, assuming that the guard is referring to the slop he has been handed.

   "No," said the guard. "How do you just sit there patiently? You are nice to me even though I keep you prisoner. Why, as a Roman citizen you shouldn't even be in here!"

   While choking down a spoonful of food, Paul considered the guard's question. "I get through it," he answered, "because I know it's God's will for me. He has given me the privilege of being here to talk to you about Jesus."

   "Did you do something wrong? Is that why you have to stay in this pit? I don't think I would consider this much of a privilege," the guard replied.

   "No," said Paul, looking around, "this part surely isn't the privilege. It's being able to talk with you that is the gift from God."

   This is a fictional account of how Paul may have handled his two-year imprisonment. How do you think he did this?

5. Paul was a witness for Jesus. You are also a witness for Jesus. What picture do people get of Jesus when they watch you? (Circle all the words that apply to you.)

   love   compassion   greed   honesty   joy   peace   conceit   strength

   faith   hope   revenge   lust   wisdom   grace   humor   pleasure

   excitement   patience   envy   bravery   self-centeredness

READ OUT LOUD

Paul returned to Jerusalem in spite of the warning he was given that there would be trouble. And as predicted, trouble found him in the form of an angry mob. You can read what happened in Acts 24:1-27.

ASK

Who do you know who acts the most like Jesus?

DISCUSS, BY THE NUMBERS

1. Paul certainly reflected the attitude of Christ when he went back to Jerusalem. And because of his bravery, God allowed Paul to go to Rome and preach the gospel there.
   - ❏ Paul stayed calm in the midst of the raging of those who accused him. **Yes.**
   - ❏ Paul secretly hated his accusers. **No, he loved his neighbor as Christ taught.**
   - ❏ Paul didn't get an attitude like his accusers. **That's right.**
   - ❏ Paul paid a hit man to kill Ananias, the high priest. **No.**
   - ❏ Paul didn't bribe while Felix wanted a bribe. **Felix kept him in prison for two years hoping for financial gain. Instead, Paul continued to share the gospel with him.**
   - ❏ Paul told the truth while his accusers lied. **Yes.**
   - ❏ Paul refused to talk badly about those who accused him while they trash-talked him. **That's right.**
   - ❏ Paul gossiped about his accusers while in jail. **No.**
2. Have fun brainstorming all kinds of cool names for Christianity, like "The Way."
3. Ask, "Why do you think it's so easy for some people to keep putting off the biggest decision of their lives—what to do with Jesus?" Ask, "Who in your immediate family keeps putting off the Jesus decision? In your extended family? Among your friends?" Ask, "How could your prayers help? How could your living like Jesus 24/7 help? How could talking with them about Jesus help?"
4. Paul refused to complain even though he remained in prison illegally for two years. He continued to talk Jesus while he was locked up. This fictional account of how Paul may have handled his two-year imprisonment can help your group members see how he thrived during these two years. He let Christ live in him and through him.
5. Examine the list of words. Talk about those that are descriptive of Jesus in our lives. Ask, "What do we need to do in order to become more like Jesus so we can more readily reflect Jesus?" This is also a great opportunity to discuss witnessing through actions.

CLOSE

In life you will be treated unfairly like Paul. So the question is, how will you respond? We learned today from Paul that, when treated unfairly, he acted differently than those who weren't Christ-followers. Paul acted like Jesus. Let's pray that God will put us in situations where we'll be shaped to be more like Jesus.

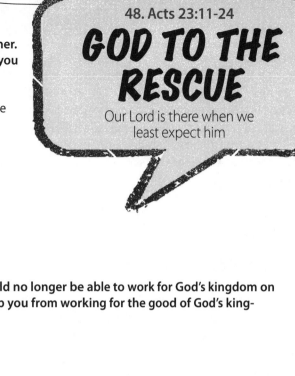

GOD TO THE RESCUE

Our Lord is there when we least expect him

1. Circle the one word that best describes what you think Paul felt while he was being held as a prisoner. Underline the one word that best describes how you feel in a crisis.

abandoned   despairing   happy   alone
confused   scared   sad   worried

2. Do you agree or disagree with this statement?

In a crisis God is always near.

❏ I agree
❏ I disagree
❏ I don't know

3. Paul faced a plot to kill him, which meant he would no longer be able to work for God's kingdom on earth. What enemy do you face who wants to stop you from working for the good of God's kingdom?

❏ Satan   ❏ My laziness
❏ My friends   ❏ My busyness
❏ Sports   ❏ School
❏ Alcohol   ❏ My family
❏ The Internet   ❏ Other: _____

4. Jamal screamed up at God in the loneliness of his bedroom. No one was home. No one was ever home. And now he had really screwed up. He had prayed, but nothing happened—nothing changed. God was nowhere to be found. God was gone. Jamal was ready to give up on this Christian stuff. It only seemed to work when things were going well. What would you tell Jamal about God being available to him and working on his behalf when things seemed to be falling apart?

5. What do you wish God would do when you face a crisis?

What do you wish God wouldn't do when you face a crisis?

What are you afraid God will do when you face a crisis?

READ OUT LOUD

In today's story Paul caps off his problems in Jerusalem by landing in prison. (Oh, and it's by an assassination plot.) Paul's situation looks bad, except for the fact that God has just told him he will be going to Rome to preach the gospel. You can read the story from Acts 23:11-24.

ASK

Who has come for a visit when you least expected that person?

DISCUSS, BY THE NUMBERS

1. Compare what they think Paul felt and what they feel in crisis. Ask, "What do you think helped Paul the most when he had a crisis like the one in today's story?" "How can you let this help you?"

2. The Bible tells us that God is always with us, yet we don't often feel God's presence when we're in the middle of a crisis. Ask, "Should we rely on our feelings during tough times, or on what God has promised us?"

3. Make a master list of all the things that block your group members from working for the good of God's kingdom. Now ask, "How do you think Paul handled these kinds of roadblocks?" "What should we do about these roadblocks?"

4. Read the situation out loud. Ask the group to answer the question, "What would you tell Jamal about God being available to him and working on his behalf when things seemed to be falling apart?"

5. Talk about the answers to each of the three questions. Answer the questions for yourself. This can help the group members see how you and God are handling tough situations.

CLOSE

It's probable that Paul wondered how God was going to keep him alive long enough to get to Rome to preach the gospel. Yet, Paul walked by faith rather than by what he could see, touch, and feel. As soon as Paul heard his nephew's story, we can be fairly certain that Paul saw how God was working, but not before then. God is a God of surprises. God is a God who often waits until the last minute. God is a God who is there when we least expect him.

EPHESUS/ SMYRNA

Sound doctrine without love/Patient endurance of suffering and persecution

1. Take this quiz to see how much you know about Christianity.

    a. What word describes the love of YHWH in the Old Testament, and what does it mean?

    b. What is the Greek word translated as Word in John 1, and what does John mean when he tells us that Jesus is the "Word"?

    c. How many judges are actually listed in the Book of Judges?

2. Jesus said the church in Ephesus did a great job at not compromising their beliefs. They didn't worship the Roman Emperor—which was required by law of all citizens. They stuck to what the Bible said. Do you know what the Bible says so that you can stick to it?

    ❏ Of course   ❏ Most of what it says

    ❏ Some of what it says   ❏ A couple of Bible stories

    ❏ Nothing

3. Which do you think is the most important?

    ❏ Holding the right Christian beliefs

    ❏ Loving God and your neighbor

    ❏ Both of these are important. You can't have one without the other.

4. The Davis family enjoyed eating dinner together. It was usually a time when they could talk about their day and have discussions about what was going on in the world.

After dinner Mr. Davis pulled out a sheet of paper from under his plate.

"We got an e-mail today from the Kirk family," he said. The Kirks were a missionary family in Morocco. The Davis family supported them through giving at their church. They had three children just like the Davises, but other than that they lived a very different life.

"Mr. Kirk says that they have increased the number of people in worship by five people," said Mr. Davis. "That doesn't sound like much unless you remember that they need to have church services in secret."

The family heard the Kirks talk about their "church" before. The services were usually held in homes and disguised as dinners or parties. It was illegal for them to worship anyone but Allah in the Muslim country they were in.

"Mrs. Kirk says that the women are still afraid to come to these churches and that her family has to be very careful to observe all the local laws," said Mrs. Davis. "She praises God for the opportunity to spread the word about Jesus."

"That would be so scary," said Matt. "The kind of trouble you get in over there is really big trouble, just for talking about Jesus."

"We need to pray that their strong faith in the Lord continues," said Mr. Davis

    How do you think the faith of Christians in some Muslim countries gets stronger even though they face extreme persecution?

5. Jesus said only good things about the church in Smyrna, nothing bad. How close is your church to the church in Smyrna? What would Jesus say about your church?

READ OUT LOUD

The church in Ephesus had all the right beliefs. They would not fall prey to false teachers, especially the Nicolaitans—a group of Christians in Ephesus who taught you could do anything you wanted because Jesus would forgive you. But they had forgotten how to love, and Jesus judged them for this.

Smyrna was a place where being a Christian was a death-defying act each and every day. If you were a member of the church in Smyrna, you lived in abject poverty—probably because committed Christians would have found it nearly impossible to make a living in a pagan culture that hated Christ-followers.

Read about both churches from Revelation 2:1-11.

ASK

How many churches would you say are in our town?

DISCUSS, BY THE NUMBERS

1. This quiz is to show what happens when you can get the right answers but don't have love. The answers are found in bold after each letter. Ask for the answers and then when your group members don't have them, say, "I'm disappointed that you couldn't get all the correct answers. What's wrong with you?" Point out that your attitude during this activity was like the church in Ephesus—they had all the right beliefs but had lost their love for God and neighbor.
   a) What word describes the love of YHWH in the Old Testament, and what does it mean? **Hesed, which means steadfast love.**
   b) What is the Greek word translated as Word in John 1, and what does John mean when he tells us that Jesus is the "Word"? **Logos. Jesus is the rational ordering principal of the universe.**
   c) How many judges are actually listed in the Book of Judges? **12—Othniel, Ehud, Shamgar, Deborah, Gideon, Tola, Jair, Jephthah, Ibzan, Elon, Abdon, Samson.**

2. Discuss the importance of knowing the epic Bible stories, popular Bible passages, and important Christian doctrines or beliefs.

3. Jesus was upset with the church in Ephesus for losing its love of God and neighbor. Read Matthew 22:35-40. Here Jesus said that all the Old Testament Law and Prophets were based on these two commandments. While they believed all the right doctrines, they forgot to love. Correct doctrine hangs on the love of God and neighbor. You must have both together. Ask, "How is it possible to believe the correct doctrine but forget love?" "How does our church sometimes do this?"

4. Talk about the Kirk family and their observations about the strong faith of the Christian citizens of the Muslim nation. See how your group members answered the question, "How do you think the faith of Christians in some Muslim countries gets stronger even though they endure persecution?"

5. In the midst of the suffering and persecution of the church in Smyrna, Jesus found nothing wrong with them. Ask, "Could the situation in Smyrna produce more committed Christians with the casual Christians dropping out?"

CLOSE

So what do these two churches have to say to our church today?

#1 The church in Ephesus reminds us that it's possible to be so preoccupied with our theology that we forget to love God and neighbor. We should never, ever let correct doctrine trump love, since all sound doctrine hangs on love. Both right beliefs and love are necessary for a healthy church to exist.

#2 The church in Smyrna lived in poverty and was persecuted, yet they remained faithful through it all. The message from Jesus—"Don't be afraid! Stick with me! You may have troubles now, but I will give you eternal life"— is the same for our church today.

PERGAMUM/THYATIRA

Religious compromise never works/Good works—bad moral standards

1. Antipas, the church bishop in Pergamum, was murdered for his faith.

Amy carried her Bible to school one day. When she dropped it two boys played keep-away with it in front of all the other kids. Is it worth it for Amy to continue to follow Jesus?

Jeff had only been at his new school for two weeks when one of the boys found out that he went to church. Since then everyone calls him "church boy." Is it worth it for Jeff to continue to follow Jesus?

Carla's friends were all going to a concert featuring a great new band. Unfortunately, Carla's dad had heard some of their lyrics and told her that they mocked God and that he didn't want her to go. How could she tell her friends that this was why she couldn't go? Is it worth it for Carla to continue to follow Jesus?

Craig thought that it would be fun to join the new Bible Club forming at school. That is, until he went the first time and all the cool kids started calling him "Jesus Geek." Is it worth it for Craig to continue to follow Jesus?

2. The Pergamum church put up with all kinds of sin because they wanted to get along with the citizens of the community who worshiped false gods. Things were so bad in the city of Pergamum that Jesus said Satan lived there. How tough do you think it was to keep your moral standards in a place like Pergamum?

❏ Nearly impossible ❏ Possible but difficult ❏ No chance

3. Do you agree (A) or disagree (D) with the following statements?

____ There will always be people around who try to get you to no longer care about sin.
____ It's okay to keep sinning because of grace.
____ Christians can do what they want, whenever they want, as long as they don't get caught.
____ It's important for Christians not to seem weird in front of nonbelievers.
____ Christians are supposed to be different than those who don't follow Jesus.

4. Doing good, but doing bad—that describes the church in Thyatira. They helped all kinds of people—the poor, the sick, the hungry. And then they went out and sinned like Satan. How easy would it be for you to do this?

❏ Easy. My good deeds make me look religious, so I can then do whatever I want.
❏ Not so easy. I like doing the good deeds but would feel guilty sinning.
❏ Other: _____

5. Jesus asked the church members in Thyatira who didn't follow the crazy teachings of Jezebel to stick to the correct teachings they had.

What are three teachings from the Bible that you will stick to?

From *More Middle School TalkSheets on the New Testament: 52 Ready-to-Use Discussions* by David Lynn. Permission to reproduce this page granted only for use in buyer's youth group. Copyright © 2010 by Youth Specialties. www.youthspecialties.com

READ OUT LOUD

Both the Pergamum church and the church at Thyatira had similar sins—they permitted false teachings, and some of their people followed them. The message given to the church at Pergamum was not to compromise theology with false teaching. The church at Thyatira's message was not to compromise morality with false teaching.

The false teachings in Pergamum were that of Balaam and the Nicolaitans—both advocating that people can sin all they want because of grace. The false teaching in Thyatira was the sin of Jezebel (a really bad person in the Old Testament)—convincing people to make bad moral choices contrary to the teachings of Jesus.

Read out loud the accounts of both churches from Revelation 2:12-29.

ASK

How often do you like to go to church?

DISCUSS, BY THE NUMBERS

1. There were people who, because of persecution, walked away from Jesus. That's why Jesus commended the church in Pergamum. They still wanted to be Christians even though their faithful bishop Antipas was roasted to death. Talk about each of the situations. Ask, "What are the benefits of continuing to follow Jesus?"

2. It was said that Satan lived in Pergamum—probably because of the Emperor worship that took place there. Talk about the question, "How tough do you think it was to keep your moral standards in a place like Pergamum?" Discuss how it is easy for the church today to tolerate sin in order to look relevant in today's society (examples include couples living together, sex outside marriage).

3. See commentary in bold after each statement.
   • There will always be people around who try to get you to no longer care about sin. **True. Just like in the church in Pergamum.**
   • It's okay to keep sinning because of grace. **No, that's part of the reason Paul wrote the book of Romans—to correct this kind of thinking.**
   • Christians can do what they want, whenever they want, as long as they don't get caught. **No way. Christians are freed from bondage to sin and freed to live for Christ. Freedom always has boundaries of protection.**
   • It's important for Christians not to seem weird in front of nonbelievers. **This can lead to a great discussion about what it means for Christians to be different versus just plain weird.**
   • Christians are supposed to be different than those who don't follow Jesus. **Yes. To live the Christian life has always meant going counter to the culture.**

4. Discuss with your group about doing both—maintaining high moral standards while caring about social justice.

5. Make a master list on flip chart paper of all the teachings your group members identify.

CLOSE

So what can we learn from these two churches? I think the followers in the church in Thyatira who didn't follow the false teaching (verses 24-25) teach us much. Jesus tells them to hold on firmly to the teachings they've already received. Can we do the same?

Loving God includes obeying God. In order to obey God's Word, we must know God's word (the church at Pergamum).

How we act matters to God (the church at Thyatira).

SARDIS/ PHILADELPHIA/ LAODICEA

All talk, no action/Trust Jesus/
No passion for Jesus

1. Which of these is true for you (if any)?

❏ I've pretended to be a Christian on Sunday but not lived for Christ the rest of the week.
❏ I've given up on being a committed Christian. I'm here because my parents make me attend.
❏ I have sometimes let the world change me rather than me changing the world for Jesus.
❏ I've tried and tried to live out my faith but keep failing.

2. The church in Sardis was filled with people who said they were Christians. But their actions said their faith was dead—that it wasn't really faith. How is your faith doing?

❏ Alive and well
❏ On life support
❏ Getting weaker
❏ Flat-lined. No brain waves whatsoever.

3. Questions Jesus might have for you if you were to visit the church in Philadelphia:

• Do you know who I am? ❏ YES ❏ NO ❏ MAYBE
• Do you know how much I love you? ❏ YES ❏ NO ❏ MAYBE
• Can this world do anything to you if I am your Lord? ❏ YES ❏ NO ❏ MAYBE
• Will you trust me? ❏ YES ❏ NO ❏ MAYBE
• Do you know that your value comes from my love for you and not from the world or the lies it is telling you? ❏ YES ❏ NO ❏ MAYBE

4. The church in Laodicea was accused by Jesus of being spiritually poor (even though they were materially wealthy), spiritually blind (even though they had an excellent eye salve), and spiritually naked (even though they were known for their woolen garments). And because of their lukewarm taste, like the lukewarm water that flowed into the city, the church in Laodicea made Jesus want to puke.

What does Jesus want to do when he tastes your church?

❏ Drink until he is thoroughly refreshed
❏ Drink half a glass
❏ Take a few sips
❏ Puke his guts out

5. Jesus saw himself knocking at the door of the Laodicean church wanting back in.

Is there evidence that Jesus is inside your church?
❏ Abundance of evidence ❏ Some evidence ❏ Lack of evidence

Is there evidence that Jesus is in your life?
❏ Abundance of evidence ❏ Some evidence ❏ Lack of evidence

READ OUT LOUD

The church at Sardis was filled with people who had the church membership card but didn't possess a genuine faith. They could talk a good talk, but their actions defied what they said. Their faith was dead.

The church at Philadelphia was promised protection by Jesus for the intense persecution that came their way. The church was promised to be made a pillar, or permanent structure, in a permanent place called heaven (unlike the temple in Jerusalem, which had been destroyed twice). And finally, Jesus promised three inscriptions would be written upon them: The name of God, which means they belong to God; the name of the city of God, which means they are citizens of heaven; and the name of Jesus, which means they possess Jesus. Like the church in Smyrna, Philadelphia was not condemned by Jesus for doing anything wrong.

The church at Laodicea was known for three things: Their wealth, because they were at the crossroads of a major trade route; their wool that made fine clothing; and their eye salve that was thought to cure many eye problems. Laodicea was also known for the cold water that came from Colosse and the mineral-rich hot springs in the nearby city of Hierapolis. The cold water came to Laodicea via stone aqueducts and was still cold when it arrived. The hot water was a different story. By the time it flowed down to Laodicea, it had turned into a tepid, lukewarm, aluminum-tasting yuck. Take a big gulp of this water and you would puke.

ASK

What is your favorite room in your church building?

DISCUSS, BY THE NUMBERS

1. See commentary in bold after each statement.
   - I've pretended to be a Christian on Sunday but not lived for Christ the rest of the week. **It's easy to do, and many Christians have been there at least once in their lives.**
   - I've given up on being a committed Christian. I'm here because my parents make me attend. **Explore how sometimes we rebel against those in authority over us—the police, the boss, the teacher, and yes, parents. This is not confined to just young** people. Adults do this, too. Ask, "How does this kind of rebellion hurt the person rebelling as well as the person being rebelled against?"
   - I have sometimes let the world change me rather than me changing the world for Jesus. **The question here is, "How can we be in the world without the world being in us?"**
   - I've tried and tried to live out my faith but keep failing. **We do this often when we use our own strength to live the Christian life. The Christian life is impossible to live. That's why Jesus sent the Holy Spirit to live in us. Living the Christian life isn't about trying harder but about yielding to Jesus.**
2. Find out where your group members saw themselves. Ask, "Is our group more like or unlike the church in Sardis?"
3. The message to the church in Philadelphia was simple: Trust Jesus. He declared to Philadelphia and to your church that he has opened a door for us that no one can shut. The world can throw any silly roadblocks it wants at us. But it can never shut the door. We are God's possessions. We have been granted citizenship in his holy city. And our Jesus makes us righteous with a righteousness the world can never take away. We can live in this truth, and fear nothing in the Lord.
4. Listen to your group's responses. Talk about what your group can do to contribute to a spiritually healthy church that tastes good to Jesus.
5. Talk about the evidence for Jesus' presence and work in your congregation and in the lives of your group members. Share some evidence of Jesus working in your life as an illustration of what it can look like for your group. Point out that Jesus is knocking—asking to be invited back into the church and into your life.

CLOSE

The churches from this passage experienced hardships and victories, just as our churches do today. Jesus' message to us is the same as it was to them—"follow me!" Let us strive to make our churches strong places where Jesus is trusted for everything.

COMING AGAIN

Why Jesus' second coming matters to you

1. Peter asked that we honestly think about what both the Old Testament prophets and New Testament apostles teach. Have you taken a serious look at what the Bible teaches?

   ❏ YES
   ❏ NO
   ❏ I'M CONFUSED

2. "Oh, brother," said Spenser as he walked out of the Sunday school room with Denny, his friend from school who had invited him.

   "What's up, Spenser?" asked Denny.

   "That whole thing about Jesus coming back and Judgment Day. My dad says we're all just going to die so we should get as much as we can while we're here. You're already dead, so how can you be punished? The stuff that teacher said is just for little kids."

   What do you think of Spenser's argument?

3. Complete this sentence stem—

   Christ has not returned yet because...

4. Mark these statements true or false—

   Jesus will return in my lifetime. _____
   I don't think much about Jesus' return. _____
   Jesus will return at night. _____
   I will be happy when Jesus returns. _____
   Jesus' return will be a big surprise. _____

5. Peter seems to say that Jesus' return can be sped up. What do you think could make Jesus come back sooner?

   ❏ I don't want Jesus to come back now.
   ❏ Praying for his return
   ❏ Telling all my friends about Jesus
   ❏ Living a holy life
   ❏ Nothing

READ OUT LOUD

Peter, one of Christ's 12 disciples, wants us to honestly think about what the Old Testament prophets and the New Testament apostles teach us about living for Jesus. In particular, how we ought to live in light of the fact of Jesus' return. Jesus promised his followers he would return soon. It's been nearly 2,000 years, and still, no Jesus. Will he really come back? Will there really be a final judgment? Will the end come as he promised? Read about it in 2 Peter 3:1-18.

ASK

When you are left home alone, do you expect your parents to return? Why?

DISCUSS, BY THE NUMBERS

This *TalkSheet* discussion is not intended to look at the specific doctrines your church believes (such as the rapture). Rather, it is intended to help your group focus on the reality of the second coming of Christ.

1. Talk with your group members about what it means to get serious with what the Scriptures teach. Does it mean you study the Bible on your own? Listen to what the sermon has to say? Get in a small group Bible study? Or just take someone else's word for what the Bible means? Or maybe just blow it off altogether?

2. It is no longer fashionable to believe in a final judgment. Many people think they are basically good, or at least their good outweighs their bad. And so there's no need for a final judgment. Or in the case of the story of Spenser, there is no life after death and therefore no need for a final judgment. Ask your group members the question, "What do you think of Spenser's argument against the second coming of Jesus and a Judgment Day?"

3. Take time to listen to your group's completed sentences. Then talk about all the reasons they came up with for Christ not returning yet. We assume that if someone doesn't keep her promise after a certain amount of time she forgot or changed plans, got too busy, or just lied. So it's easy to see why people would think that Christ would do the same. Yet, Peter is clear in today's story that God is on a different timetable than we are. A thousand days and one day are the same to him. He is the great "I AM" who was and is and is to come. And he is patiently waiting for more people to be saved before he sends Jesus back.

4. See commentary in bold after each statement.
   - Jesus will return in my lifetime. **We don't know. Scripture is clear. We won't know, so quit trying to figure out when—be it the day, the month, the year, or the century. Instead, focus on what you should be doing for Jesus because he will return some day.**
   - I don't think much about Jesus' return. **We need to reflect on his return as a reminder of how we should live in the present.**
   - Jesus will return at night. Again, we don't know. **Night is assumed because a thief robs at night. But thieves also rob during the daylight hours.**
   - I will be happy when Jesus returns. **We hope so!**
   - Jesus' return will be a big surprise. **That's what Scripture says.**

5. Since God is patiently working out his purpose that more and more people will be saved, Peter may mean that we can help accomplish these purposes faster by cooperating with God in telling others the good news, praying that God's purposes will be achieved, and living a holy life. Another interpretation is that we don't dread the second coming but anxiously await and welcome it. Listen to the completed sentences and dialogue with your group members about the two possible meanings of this passage.

CLOSE

Maranatha, a term used by the early church that means "Our Lord is coming" or "Come Lord Jesus," is a word we can use today. Say the word, *Maranatha*, and remember that this word calls us to live each day in light of Jesus' promised return.

Share Your Thoughts

With the Author: Your comments will be forwarded to the author when you send them to *zauthor@zondervan.com*.

With Zondervan: Submit your review of this book by writing to *zreview@zondervan.com*.

Free Online Resources at
www.zondervan.com

Zondervan AuthorTracker: Be notified whenever your favorite authors publish new books, go on tour, or post an update about what's happening in their lives at www.zondervan.com/authortracker.

Daily Bible Verses and Devotions: Enrich your life with daily Bible verses or devotions that help you start every morning focused on God. Visit www.zondervan.com/newsletters.

Free Email Publications: Sign up for newsletters on Christian living, academic resources, church ministry, fiction, children's resources, and more. Visit www.zondervan.com/newsletters.

Zondervan Bible Search: Find and compare Bible passages in a variety of translations at www.zondervanbiblesearch.com.

Other Benefits: Register yourself to receive online benefits like coupons and special offers, or to participate in research.

ZONDERVAN®

ZONDERVAN.com/
AUTHORTRACKER
follow your favorite authors